THE PIANO
A Pictorial Account of Its Ancestry and Development

Birthday Greetings to Moravian Bishop van Vleck. Painting, anonymous, USA, 1795 (Moravian Historical Society, Nazareth, Pennsylvania). This Moravian group is gathered around a stringed keyboard instrument drawn out of scale and appearing gigantic. The unskilled artist omitted important details but a clavichord was surely intended.

Ambrose Andrews Schuyler Family. Painting by an unknown American artist, c. 1824 (The New-York Historical Society). This portrait of an American family, the work of an unschooled painter, shows them seated around their square piano. The piano is painted as carefully as the members of the family, the bottom key correctly shown as FF which it would typically have been at this time. The artist, however, planned his space poorly and was unable to show the top note as f^3 although the total length of the keyboard is roughly equivalent to the expected five octaves, judging from the space allotted to the lowest octave. The prominence given to the piano in the composition suggests it was a family treasure.

THE PIANO

A PICTORIAL ACCOUNT OF
ITS ANCESTRY AND DEVELOPMENT

HELEN RICE HOLLIS

HIPPOCRENE
BOOKS, INC.

To Anne and Richard and S.Y.

For information write to:
Hippocrene Books
171 Madison Avenue
New York N.Y. 10016

Library of Congress Catalog Card Number 74-30924
ISBN 0-88254-324-5

Printed in Great Britain

CONTENTS

		page
	Acknowledgements	6
	Introduction	8
1	Earliest ancestors	11
2	Clavichords	17
3	Harpsichords	25
4	The transition to piano	47
5	Pianos	51
6	In America	88
7	Stringed keyboard instruments today	112
	Notes and references	115
	Selective bibliography	117
	Index	120

ACKNOWLEDGEMENTS

To list all of the friends and colleagues from whom I have received information, help, encouragement, or all three, would seem presumptuous, but the following must be specifically mentioned—they are, of course, blameless for any of my sins of commission or omission:

Frank Hubbard, for reading at one stage the section on harpsichords and making valuable criticism and suggestions; John Steinway for the same great favor in regard to the piano; Edwin M. Ripin for similar attention to the material on the clavichord and the early piano, especially, and also for pointing out several works of art that had escaped my attention; Dr Clement M. Miller and Dr Howard M. Brown for opening my eyes to the value and pleasure of iconography of musical instruments—the important studies in this area by Dr Emanuel Winternitz have, of course, been a revelation to all.

The encouragement of my children Anne Hollis Reese and Richard Avery Hollis, and members of the Smithsonian Institution staff, especially Virginia Beets and Richard Ahlborn, has kept the project from floundering on more than one occasion; and C. Malcolm Watkins, chairman of the Department of Cultural History, Smithsonian Institution, gave me reassurance and support when it was most needed.

I am infinitely grateful to a friend, who wishes to remain unnamed, for patiently reading the manuscript and making perceptive suggestions for clarification of certain material to the layman.

ILLUSTRATIONS

My thanks are due to John Fesperman, supervisor and curator of the Division of Musical Instruments, Smithsonian Institution, for permission to use photographs from the division archives and to the various museums and private collectors for permitting me to use photographs of instruments and works of art in their collections and for providing information on them.

The late Canon Colin Stephenson, formerly Master of the College of Guardians, Shrine of Our Lady of Walsingham, and Canon of Norwich Cathedral, England, made an extraordinary contribution and gesture of friendship by assisting me to obtain a photograph taken from scaffolding of Manchester Cathedral of the angel harpsichordist (plate 22). It is probably the first time that this sculpture, often mentioned in references, has been successfully photographed. Special thanks are due to Dr Hans Grüss, Karl Marx Universität, Leipzig, for the photograph of the action of the Cristofori piano. The painting in plate 42 was reproduced by permission of Captain

Evelyn Broadwood and Broadwood & Sons; and plates 51, 78, by that of Im Urs Graf-Verlag, Switzerland.

The majority of prints were supplied by the collections, libraries and museums in which the instruments are housed. The following exceptions apply: plates 10, 15, Gabinetto Fotografico Nazionale, Rome; 12, 13, 21, Royal Commission on Historical Monuments, National Monuments Record, London; 22, Perfecta Publications Ltd; 5, 23, 24, 28, 46, Photographie Giraudon, Paris; 25, Lichtbildwerkstätte 'Alpenland', Vienna; 42, Royal Academy of Arts, London; 47, 48, Musée Instrumental du Conservatoire National de Musique, Paris; 56, A. C. Cooper Fine Art Photographer, London; 97, 99, Steinway & Sons; half-title photograph, Smithsonian Institution; page 65, Victoria & Albert Museum.

INTRODUCTION

This book is planned as a pictorial addition to the considerable number of works on the piano that explore its ancestry, history and the technical aspects of its development.

To any serious student of the history of the piano Rosamond E. M. Harding's *The Piano-forte: Its History Traced to the Great Exhibition of 1851* is indispensable. Arthur Loesser in his entertaining and readable work *Men, Women and Pianos* enlivened and humanised the subject, carrying it up to the twentieth century. In my studies I have found it a valuable companion to the Harding work. Nevertheless an up-to-date history of the piano, combining the scholarship of Harding with the imagination and wit of Loesser, is long overdue.

As to my own work, I see it as a useful companion to the books mentioned above and to other studies. My aim has been to enhance and amplify the subject with pictorial material, both serious and light-hearted, accompanied by enough text to link the illustrations in a general historical account. Throughout I have tried to clarify and simplify terminology, keeping in mind the reader who is more interested in how and why the piano came about and its effect on musical and social life than in how to make one.

The illustrations may provide useful reference material for students of the subject as well as for social historians. They fall into two categories: photographs of musical instruments, and photographs of works of art in which instruments are shown. The first group reflects milestones in the development of the piano and a few unsuccessful experiments in the application of a keyboard to a stringed instrument. As to the works of art, they are included as a valuable source of information on musical instruments through the ages. For instance, saints and angels in medieval and Renaissance art often play real contemporary instruments in convincing ensembles. So do allegorical or classical figures in the Renaissance (although less dependably), and by the seventeenth century one finds ensemble groups represented in 'true concert scenes with professional or amateur performers . . . reliable enough to be analysed by the musicologist for performance techniques'.[1]

Works of art, on the whole better preserved than the instruments themselves, often furnish evidence of instruments now lost or indicate the existence or prevalence of certain types earlier than we had been inclined to believe. Music historians find that the forms of instruments, the manner and the combinations in which they were used, their importance and the esteem in which they were held, the kind of people who played them and the social settings of the occasions, are sometimes revealed more tellingly in sculpture or painting than in descriptive accounts. Flemish and Dutch painters of the seventeenth century, in particular, have left us a notably rich record of domestic musical life of the period. They show instruments with such careful attention to details that in a few instances we can even identify with some degree of certainty the maker of an instrument depicted (see plate 30).

If, however, a musical instrument in a work of art cannot be verified by other evidence, ie a surviving instrument or a written text, the artist is suspect of having invented, indulged in fantasy or poorly observed his subject. Therefore, whether the artist's approach is symbolic, allegorical, scientific or humanistic, his work must be carefully considered before any conclusion or even reasonable conjecture can be made as to its validity as musicological study material.

A case in point is a group of representations of clavichords shown in the following pages. Later examples, with the strings tuned to different pitches and visible raised soundboards at their right ends, are, of course, familiar to us from numerous extant examples. Yet early artists in various countries depicted instruments in which the strings were all in unison and the soundboards, if there were any, must have extended beneath the keys. No such instruments are known to have survived.

This material presents a problem—can one trust it? Documentary evidence of their having once existed is provided, however, by Henri Arnault in his fifteenth-century treatise on musical instruments. He shows a layout of a clavichord indicating that the strings are all at the same pitch and, in describing its construction, speaks of an 'upper' and a 'lower bottom'. Upper bottom almost certainly refers to a soundboard under the keys. Thus Arnault's treatise corroborates art works of his time.

Predecessors of the piano receive considerable attention. Some of these art works are as irresistible as they are little known, but beyond their aesthetic appeal or diversionary charm, they remind us how much creative energy and loving labor have been devoted to producing fine keyboard instruments for more than five centuries.

Both direct and indirect antecedents of the piano are shown on the following pages—the struck strings as well as the plucked strings. The harp, the psaltery, and the dulcimer—all of great antiquity—are the founders of the family. The harp and psaltery, plucked with fingers or plectra, are close relatives of the harpsichord. The strings of the dulcimer are struck with small mallets or hammers, giving it a claim to kinship with the clavichord and piano. Psalteries and dulcimers are composed of strings stretched above attached soundboards. The harpsichord may be thought of therefore as a mechanized psaltery, the clavichord and piano as mechanized dulcimers.

Does the harpsichord really belong here then? While the clavichord is always cited as the true ancestor of the piano, since both play by striking strings, the first piano was made by a harpsichord-maker in an attempt to increase the resources of his instrument. Furthermore, since it was the harpsichord that the piano replaced as the all-purpose keyboard instrument in the eighteenth century, it must take part in any consideration of the events leading up to the development and ascendancy of the piano.

The organistrum (later to become the hurdy-gurdy), not always accorded consideration as a member of this family, is included too, since it represents the earliest stringed instrument with a keyboard.

The shortened word, piano, is used throughout. Bartolomeo Cristofori, the inventor of the instrument, called it *gravicembalo col piano e forte*—harpsichord with soft and loud. Although pianoforte became and remains its proper name, and at times other designations such as forte-piano and Hammerklavier (Beethoven's chauvinistic preference) have been tried, the abbreviated term is now accepted and used in most languages.

I

EARLIEST ANCESTORS

Harps of one kind or another of many sizes and shapes were known in most early civilisations. The addition of a soundboard to a harp produces a psaltery or a dulcimer. These, too, appear in many different forms (plates 1–5).

Keyboards attached to organs made their appearance early in history—Hero of Alexandria described an organ with a keyboard in the third century BC—and the application of a keyboard to a stringed instrument was described as early as the tenth century by St Odo who wrote of the organistrum, a remarkably ingenious instrument in which several strings rest against a resined wheel. The wheel is turned by a crank setting the strings in vibration, much as does the bow on the strings of a violin. Some of the organistrum's strings are unstopped, providing a drone accompaniment to a melody played on a small keyboard of some kind that causes tangents to press against other strings. The tangent mechanism is similar to the simple mechanism of the clavichord and indeed may have suggested it.

In the twelfth century the organistrum is depicted as a large fiddle-shaped instrument that required two people to play—one to turn the wheel and the other to stop the strings. Later types (plates 6, 7) are played by a single person. We know the organistrum today as the hurdy-gurdy.

PLATE I

Angel playing a psaltery. Sculpture in marble by Andrea Orcagna, Italy, c. 1308–68 (The Norton Simon Foundation, Fullerton, California). Here the psaltery appears to be held by a band around the angel's shoulders as he plucks the strings with the index finger of the left hand while the right hand uses a long quill as a plectrum. The psaltery is sometimes held with one hand while the other plays. Elsewhere one sees it held on the lap or set on a table leaving both hands free to play.

PLATE 2

Madonna and child in a closed garden. Colored woodcut, anonymous German, Swabian or Franconian, c. 1450–70 (National Gallery of Art, Washington, DC, Rosenwald Collection). The angel (right) plucks the strings of the psaltery with several fingers of each hand while supporting the instrument by resting its in-curved sides on the crooks of his bent elbows.

PLATE 5

Dulcimer player, page from an illuminated manuscript entitled *Le livre des échecs amoureux*, France, sixteenth century Bibliothèque Nationale, Paris, ms fr 143. The lady is holding two light crook-shaped hammers for striking the strings. Psalteries and dulcimers appear in a variety of shapes, but the details are usually indistinguishable except for the manner in which they are played. When the strings are plucked the instrument is a psaltery; when they are struck it is a dulcimer. Musicians in the background play pipe and tabor, shawm, and bagpipes, and sing from a manuscript. A small harp, a portative organ, and a recorder rest on the floor. The dulcimer survives today as a folk instrument in many countries. In Rumania and Hungary it is *cimbalom*, in Iran *santur*, in Greece *santouri*. It is found in America in scattered communities of European origin where folk practices of the mother country are still remembered.

PLATE 7
Hurdy-gurdy by Joseph (?) Bassot, France, eighteenth century (Smithsonian Institution, 94,866). The term organistrum was supplanted in the fourteenth century by other names such as symphonie, armonie, vielle, Leier, and by hurdy-gurdy in eighteenth-century England. Its social status was also variable. Seen played by angels or saints in its early life, it is spoken of as a beggar's instrument in the seventeenth century, but in eighteenth-century France it again became 'respectable' and was played by noblemen and aristocrats.

The hurdy-gurdy shown here possesses two chanterelles or melody strings stopped by wooden keys, and four unstopped drone strings.

PLATE 6 (*above left*)
Angel with an organistrum. Sculpture in marble by Andrea Orcagna, Italy, c. 1308–64 (National Gallery of Art, Washington, DC, Samuel H. Kress Collection). Hero of Alexandria described a hydraulic organ with a keyboard, in the third century BC, but the organistrum is the earliest form of a stringed instrument provided with a keyboard. It is described by Saint Odo of Cluny in the tenth century and depicted as early as the twelfth century as a large fiddle-shaped instrument that required two people to play—one to turn the wheel and one to stop the strings.

The crank turns a resined wheel which presses against the strings setting them in vibration. The tangents operated by the keys then stop the strings, as do a violinist's fingers, to play a melody. In this sculpture the keys are round buttons played with one hand while the other hand turns the wheel—a one-person operation which became standard. The tangent mechanism is similar to the simple mechanism of the clavichord and indeed may have suggested it.

2

CLAVICHORDS

The clavichord was derived from the application of a keyboard to the monochord—a mathematical more than a musical instrument that was used by Greek philosophers, notably Pythagoras, for investigating the nature of musical sound. In the eleventh century, Guido of Arezzo employed the monochord to indicate the eight tones of the ecclesiastical modes on which the plainsong of the Church was based.

The terms monochord, manichordion, and manichord seem early to have been used interchangeably to denote the device described above or the instrument we now call 'clavichord', a word which first appeared in 1404 in the rules for the Minnesingers.

The mechanism of the clavichord is of the utmost simplicity. Each key has an upright metal tangent attached to its rear end; when a key is depressed its tangent strikes metal strings—usually a pair for each note. Felt strips are threaded between the strings at their left ends to prevent that portion from vibrating; the sounding lengths of the strings (ie the pitch determinants) are the distances between the points at which the tangents touch them and the bridge at the right.

Since the tangent remains in contact with the strings as long as the key is held down the sound produced is very small, but the clavichord is peculiarly touch sensitive and is capable of gradation of dynamics within a small range and of a delicate vibrato (*Bebung*). The latter is an effect unique among keyboard instruments and is possible because the performer may vary the pressure of the key he is holding down, thereby varying the pressure of the tangent on the strings to cause a subtle fluctuation of pitch as well as to prolong the vibration (plate 8).

The small sound and subtle expression of the clavichord preclude its use as an ensemble or accompanying instrument. It is an instrument to play for one's solitary pleasure or for friends in an intimate setting (plates 16, 17).

It is not known or likely to be known just where the first clavichords were made but descriptions suggesting some sort of stringed keyboard instrument exist in Burgundian, French, English and Spanish writings as early as the fourteenth century. Makers of harpsichords are known to have been working in Italy as early as 1419. Indications from works of art are clear, however, that by the mid-fifteenth century, clavichords and harpsichords were rather widely known on the European continent[2] as well as the British Isles. The variety of media of these representations is as striking as their widespread provenances (plates 9–14).

The early representations of clavichords show instruments, the strings of which are in unison and on which no soundboard is visible. There has

Fig. 1
A woodcut of a monochord in *Musica Theorica* by Lodovico Fogliano, published in Venice in 1529

been speculation as to whether a soundboard may have run under the keys and indeed the presence of a soundboard is indicated in a drawing in Henri Arnault's remarkable fifteenth-century treatise on musical instruments (plate 11) and in his notes which speak of the upper and lower bottoms. A painting by a follower of the 'Master of the Half Lengths' (plate 17) shows a clavichord with a soundboard clearly visible under the keys.

The earliest clavichords were fretted (*gebunden*), ie one pair of strings served for several keys (plate 18a). Only at a later date were clavichords made in which two or even three strings were provided for each key—unfretted (*bundfrei*) (plate 18b).

Toward the end of the fifteenth century, strings tuned to different pitches began to appear on clavichords (plate 15) and ultimately the instrument was lengthened to accommodate a larger soundboard at the right end.

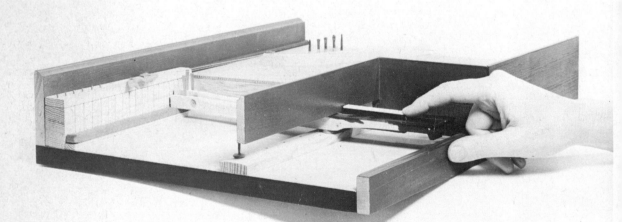

PLATE 8

Model of clavichord action (Smithsonian Institution). The middle tangent on the end of the key that is being depressed is striking its pair of strings.

PLATE 9

Altarpiece from cathedral
(*right*) from the cathedral
at Minden, Germany, 1425
(Bodemuseum, Berlin, Ger-
man Democratic Repub-
lic). The earliest representation of the clavichord and
harpsichord at present
known are seen in this
sculpture in the section of
the border just below right
center. No explanation is
offered for the bass strings
being on the wrong side
of the harpsichord either
in this or the Kefermarkt
sculpture in plate 25.

PLATE 10

Fresco by Leonardo da Besozzo, Naples, c. 1428[3] (Caracciolo Chapel of San Giovanni a Carbonara, Naples, Italy). The primitive clavichord here (accompanied by psaltery and bells) has no visible soundboard.

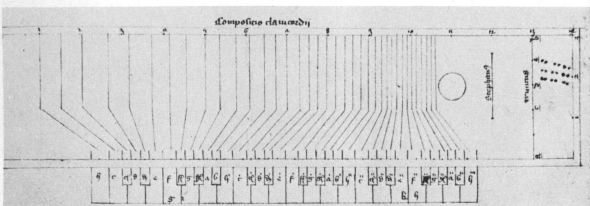

PLATE 11

Portion of a page from the treatise on musical instruments by Henri Arnault de Zwolle, c. 1440 (Bibliothèque Nationale, Paris, ms fonds Latin 7295). This page shows the layout of a clavichord. Arnault gives directions for determining the sounding lengths of the strings. As with other clavichords of early date, the strings are tuned in unison and the soundboard, a part of which is visible, may extend beneath the keys as Arnault's notes seem to indicate.

PLATE 12

Clavichord represented in stained glass window designed by John Prudde, commissioned 1441 (St Mary's Church, Warwick, England).

PLATE 13

Angel playing a clavichord. Sculpture in wood, before 1471. (Church of St Mary, Shrewsbury, England). This crude sculpture is an attempt to represent a fretted clavichord. More keys than strings are indicated.

PLATE 14

Page from *Weimarer Ingenieurkunst und Wunderbuch* (*Weimar Engineering Art and Miracle Book*) (Thuringische Landesbibliothek, Weimar, Germany, ms fol 328). This naive drawing of a harpsichord and clavichord is shown as much for the questions it raises as for the information it furnishes. It is often reproduced and has been dated c. 1440. According to Konrad Marwinski, Chief of the Department of Information and Special Collections, Weimar Library, this date is in doubt; he finds that the manuscript is the work of several hands, that the style of clothing points to the first half of the sixteenth century and that there appears in the manuscript a portrait of Maximilian I (1459–1519). He adds, however, that the 1440 date has some relevance in that many of the drawings in the codex are copies of others done some 100 years earlier.[4] The exact date, then, remains conjectural.

The illustrator has neglected to show bridges or mechanisms for the instruments and has drawn keyboards with each narrow key set between a pair of wider ones—an unlikely arrangement even for an early diatonic keyboard. Obviously, the instruments as shown could not function, but the same keyboard plan is said to be visible in a manuscript preserved in the public library of Ghent, Belgium, and believed to date from the fourteenth century.

PLATE 15 (*facing page, below*)

Intarsia, between 1479 and 1482, showing a clavichord from the Ducal Palace, Urbino, Italy. Edwin Ripin sees in this sophisticated representation of a clavichord in intarsia a 'transitional' instrument, its low soundboard probably extending beneath the keys as in the preceding examples, but its strings turned to different pitches rather than in unison. With forty-seven keys and seventeen strings, it obviously represents a fretted instrument.[5]

PLATE 16

Woman playing a clavichord. Painting attributed to Jan van Hemessen, Flemish, 1500–66 (Worcester Art Museum, Worcester, Massachusetts). This charming scene gives an excellent impression of the intimacy associated with the clavichord. Its tone is so delicate that it is ideal only for solitary musical self-communion, or to be played for a small group in an intimate setting.

PLATE 17

Woman with a clavichord. Painting by a follower of the Master of the Female Half-lengths, Flemish, c. 1535–40 (Collection of Adelyn D. Breeskin, Washington, DC). Here one sees how easily a small clavichord could be moved around to be put on a table or stand for use. A soundboard is visible beneath the keys.

23

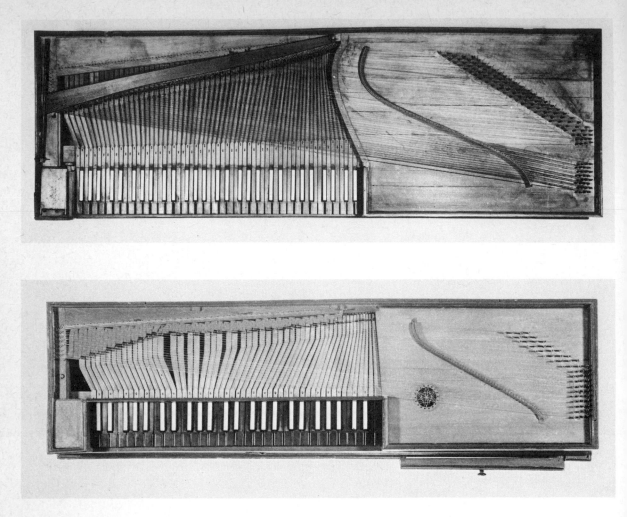

PLATES 18a and 18b

Plan views of two clavichords. (*Top*) Germany, eighteenth century (Smithsonian Institution, 60,1394, formerly Cooper Union Collection); (*bottom*) by Johann Michael Voit, Schweinfurth, Germany, 1812 (Smithsonian Institution, 303,542, Hugo Worch Collection). These two views show the arrangements of the keys of a fretted and an unfretted clavichord. They also show the change from the earlier examples which have unison strings of equal lengths and soundboards extending under the keys, to a design with strings graduated in length and gauge and a more effective soundboard raised at the right end.

The upper instrument is fretted, which accounts for the angling of the rear of the keys; the seemingly erratic spacing is necessary because some pairs of keys must strike the same pairs of strings. The lower instrument is unfretted—each key has its own pair of strings. It was a large unfretted clavichord on which Carl Phillip Emmanuel Bach's playing deeply moved his contemporaries. In earlier examples as many as four keys struck the same pair of strings.

3

HARPSICHORDS

The harpsichord, virginal and spinet[6] make their music by plucking metal strings from a keyboard. An upright jack of wood equipped with a plectrum in a pivoted tongue rests on the rear end of each key. When a key is depressed the jack travels up and the plectrum plucks a string en route. With the release of the key the jack falls and the plectrum, thanks to the pivoted tongue, barely touches the string without any audible sound on its way back down. Each jack has its own small felt damper that rests on the string until the key is struck and lifts as the string is plucked to permit its vibration as long as the key is held down.

A wooden bar is suspended from the sides of the frame above the jacks to prevent their jumping up out of place. The underside of this jack-rail is cushioned with felt to deaden the noise of the jacks hitting against it (plate 19).

One or several strings are played from one or two (in rare examples, three) keyboards, this variation made possible by stops or other arrangements to shift the jacks from playing to non-playing position. The plectra are most often of crow quill, but sometimes of cowhide or buffalo skin.

The harpsichord speaks with a clarity that makes it ideally suitable for delineating parts in a polyphonic texture or for playing a chordal accompaniment to a melody. While graded dynamics are impossible to achieve by varying the pressure on the keys, this may be accomplished by the structure of the music itself. The great harpsichord-composers cannily built up or diminished the volume of sound by altering the spacing of the parts or, by adding or subtracting notes to thicken or thin the texture. In performance a note may be emphasized by ornamenting it with a trill or a turn, or prolonged by repeating it or extending the trill.

The rich sonority of the harpsichord is fully revealed by the composers of its solo literature. For the terrace dynamics or echo effects of some Baroque music, the instrument with two keyboards and several sets of strings is especially suitable. Such a harpsichord characteristically has two sets of strings at 'normal' (ie 8') pitch and one set tuned an octave higher (4'). (Only rarely does it have a set at 16' or one at 2' pitch (one octave below, or two above, normal pitch).[7]

An elusive keyboard instrument, the échiquier,[8] existed along with the clavichord and harpsichord in the sixteenth century. The word seems not to have been simply another name for one of these, since échiquier and *épinette* (harpsichord) appear together in sixteenth-century documents. The échiquier is mentioned also as an accompaniment to dancing for which the sound of a clavichord is too delicate.

It is possibly the instrument described by Henri Arnault in the last of his four plans for making a clavisymbalom, as follows:

> This key has a piece attached to its upper part and leaded so that when the key is struck and strikes against an obstacle above near the strings this piece is projected in the direction of the strings, and, after having touched them, falls back, given that the key is held down.[9]

This is remarkably suggestive of the escapement of the piano action and tantalizing since no such instrument or representation of it is known to have survived. One of the terms used for it is *eschaquier d'Angleterre*, inviting the conjecture that it may have originated or was especially popular in England.

As mentioned previously, the earliest depiction of a harpsichord now known dates from 1425 (plate 9) and the manuscript of Henri Arnault (plate 20) c. 1440 not only gives a layout of a harpsichord but also describes four possible ways of constructing the plucking mechanism.

The harpsichord was to assume a number of sizes and shapes and to acquire some sophisticated refinements. The larger instruments were played in palaces and great houses, in concert, theatre and church performances, the spinets and virginals in domestic settings. In art one sees it in both angelic and earthly settings (plates 21–50).

PLATE 19

Model of harpsichord action (detail) (Smithsonian Institution). This shows jack-slides from which some jacks have been removed. The plectrum of the jack on the left in front is about to pluck the string as the key on which it stands is depressed. The jack behind this has its plectrum pointing in the other direction and only the rear end of it can be seen. The other jacks are at rest, their felt dampers sitting on the strings. Above can be seen a section of the jack-rail with its felt padding.

PLATE 20

Page from the treatise on musical instruments by Arnault de Zwolle c. 1440 (Bibliothèque Nationale, Paris, ms fonds Latin 7295). On this page Arnault shows the layout of a wing-shaped keyboard instrument accompanied by detailed drawings of jacks, and gives instructions for four methods of constructing a clavisymbalom. The treatise is in 'dog Latin', full of abbreviations and difficult to read, but the systems, as well as they can be understood, seem workable, although at least one of them is highly cumbersome. In one plan the strings are struck rather than plucked (see the description of the fourth plan on p 26), indicating that Arnault was using the word clavisymbalom to include more than one type of stringed keyboard instrument. The French translators of the manuscript[10] found evidence that Arnault was describing instruments actually in existence during his time rather than theorizing about how one might make a musical instrument. With his plan for a clavichord (plate 11), these are among the earliest-known representations of the 'modern' form of the keyboard with accidentals in twos and threes.

The exact date that the chromatic keyboard came into use is unknown, but it is seen as early as c. 1426 on an organ played by St Cecilia in a painting by Hubert and Jan van Eyck in St Bavon Cathedral, Ghent.

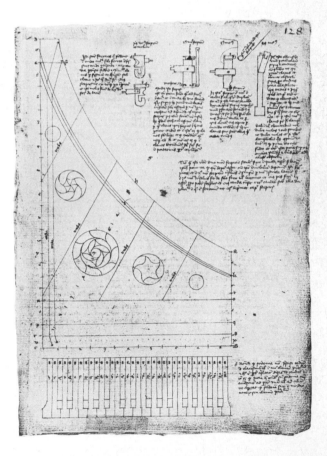

PLATE 21 (*above left*)

Harpsichord in a stained glass window designed by John Prudde, commissioned 1441 (St Mary's Church, Warwick, England).

PLATE 22 (*above right*)

Angel playing a harpsichord. Sculpture in wood, c. 1465 (ceiling of the nave of Manchester Cathedral, England). Here the sculptor has planned the perspective with consideration for the fact that the angel must be seen from far below, and he has shown the harpsichord quite accurately in spite of the difficulty presented by his medium. The bridge and jacks are indicated and the keyboard shows accidentals raised above the naturals and grouped, albeit the spacing is curious.

PLATE 23 (*right*)

'La cour céleste devant la vièrge et le fils',—page by Jean Colombe from *Les très riches heures du Duc du Berry*, c. 1485 (Musée de Condé, Chantilly, France, ms fol 126). In the lower right-hand corner an angel plays a carefully drawn harpsichord. Others play lute, rebecs, recorders and portative organ.

PLATE 24

'Singe au claveçin', detail from a fifteenth-century French manuscript, *L'histoire de la conqueste du noble et riche toison d'or* (Bibliothèque Nationale, Paris, ms 1295). Rosamond E. M. Harding[11] is inclined to the opinion that the instrument shown here is a keyed dulcimer. If this is so, it would then be the earliest representation of a piano-type known. There is, however, no evidence of hammers, but, rather, behind the keyboard a bar suggestive of a harpsichord jack-rail. It has been offered as a possible candidate for the third of Henri Arnault's plans for a clavisymbalom: 'In this jack system . . . the keys are higher than the wrest plank.'[12] It is safer to view this illustration as amusing rather than informative.

29

PLATE 25

Sculpture 1490–8 (parish church of Kefermarkt, upper Austria). This sculpture is the earliest known representation of an upright harpsichord or clavicytherium; it is played by an angel while two others play shawm and lute. Virdung includes a description and sketch of the clavicytherium in his *Musica Getutscht* (1511) and states that it was strung with gut strings.

PLATE 26

Clavicytherium; compass C/E to g³, 1 × 8′ (Royal College of Music, London, Donaldson Collection).[7] This is said to be the earliest existing upright harpsichord. Believed to date from the last twenty years of the fifteenth century,[13] it may therefore be the oldest extant stringed keyboard instrument of any type. Instead of the familiar structure of the soundboard, the narrow soundboard is supported by the bentside and an almost parallel inner bentside. A sculptured landscape of softwood suggesting a north Italian style is applied to the back; but a fragment of a lease contracted at Ulm and pasted over a split in the back of the instrument suggest it may have been used and possibly even made in Swabia. The instrument has been exactly copied except for the ornamentation by a fine English harpsichord-builder. The sophisticated action works flawlessly and the tone is sweet and ringing.

PLATE 27

Plan view of a virginal by an unknown Italian maker, Italy, sixteenth or seventeenth century; compass[7] C/E to c³ (Smithsonian Institution, 303,545, Hugo Worch Collection). The smaller plucked stringed keyboard instruments included the virginals—polygonal or rectangular—operating in the same manner as the harpsichord, but possessing only one set of strings. The virginal shown here is tuned according to a system known as 'short octave' tuning. This was an idea carried over from organ building where it was an economy measure, the long low-pitched pipes being expensive in material and labor.

For most music through the seventeenth century the lowest accidentals were non-essential and were often omitted on keyboard instruments of the time. The most common were the C and the G short octaves. In the former, indicated C/E, the lowest key which appears to be E sounds C, the F♯ key sounds D and the G♯, E. In the G short octave indicated as GG/BB, apparent BB sounds GG, apparent C♯ and D♯ sound AA and BB respectively.

Early virginal music often contains widely spaced chords possible to play only on a short octave instrument.

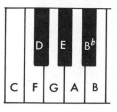 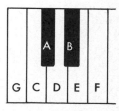

Fig. 2
Arrangement of keys of short octave keyboards

PLATE 28 (*above*)

Concert Champêtre, anonymous, Italy, sixteenth century (Musée du Berry, Bourges, France). Here an Italian virginalist is playing *basso continuo*[14] in company with viola da gamba, lute, and recorder. The virginal is remarkably similar to the one in the preceding plate, although, apparently, clumsy repainting has disarranged its keys and obliterated the strings of the lute.

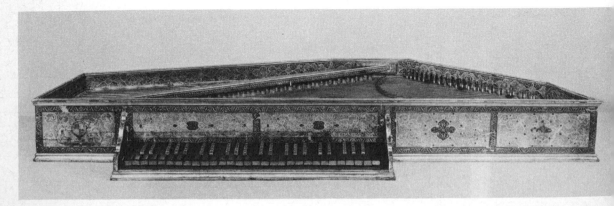

PLATE 29 (*facing page, below*)

Polygonal virginal, Italy, sixteenth century; compass GG/BB to c³ (Victoria and Albert Museum, London, 19–1887). The virginal shown here has long been known as Queen Elizabeth's; on the left panel are the arms borne by Henry IV and successive monarchs until Elizabeth's death in 1603, and on the right the badge, a falcon crowned and holding a sceptre, used by both Anne Boleyn and her daughter. The instrument is unsigned but is certainly of Italian origin, and probably of the late sixteenth century. It is one of the most sumptuous of virginals and worthy of a queen. Its front face is elaborately decorated with arabesques painted in gold on panels of red surrounded by green borders. The inside of the hinged front section of the outer case is built to serve as a music desk—an unusual feature. The inner surface is painted with foliage in gold on a gold-sprinkled black ground. The natural keys are ebony-topped with gilded fronts and the accidentals are inlaid with ivory, silver and various woods. The outer case is covered with crimson velvet and lined with yellow satin.

Her contemporaries reported that Queen Elizabeth played the virginal with both pleasure and competence. The extensive collection of her father, Henry VIII, himself an enthusiastic musician, included an astonishing number of keyboard instruments: virginals, clavichords, regals, claviorgana and an instrument described in the Privy Purse expenses of 1530 as a pair of virginals in one coffer with four stops—an early two-manual harpsichord.

The virginal was called 'virginals' or 'pair of virginals' in the sixteenth century, the word pair being applied to complex musical instruments (ie pair of bagpipes, organs, clavichords, virginals, etc). The origin of the term is a matter for speculation, and several theories are advanced. The most convincing seems to be that it was an instrument thought 'proper for girls' (from the Latin *virginalis*), the lute, considered more difficult to play, being reserved as the 'manly' instrument. I have come across only one painting, Italian, showing a man seated at a virginal, but there are many representations of young women picturesquely standing or (rarely) seated at virginals. Shakespeare commemorates them in his sonnet number 128:

How oft, when thou, my music play'st,
Upon that blessed wood whose motion sounds
With thy sweet fingers, when thou gently sway'st
The wiry concord that mine ear confounds,
Do I envy those jacks that nimble leap
To kiss the tender inward of thy hand,
Whilst my poor lips, which should that harvest reap,
At the wood's boldness by thee blushing stand!
To be so tickled, they would change their state
And situation with those dancing chips,
O'er whom thy fingers walk with gentle gait,
Making dead wood more blest than living lips.
  Since saucy jacks so happy are in this,
  Give them thy fingers, me thy lips to kiss.

It seems the poet confused the mechanics of the virginal; the jacks of the instrument can hardly, 'nimbly leap to kiss the tender inward of thy hand'.

PLATE 31 (*left*)

Woman Receiving a Virginal Lesson. Painting by Jan Vermeer, 1632–75 (Windsor Castle Collection, Berkshire, England). This typical seventeenth-century Dutch domestic scene shows a woman standing to play a Flemish virginal. It was customary for makers to apply ornamental block-printed paper to the cases of virginals. The paper with a design of confronting seahorses as seen in this painting was often, if not exclusively, used by members of the Ruckers family (see preceding plate). Dutch masters of the seventeenth century painted many scenes of young women playing virginals, in concert with other instruments such as lutes, guitars, violins, cellos or viole da gamba and flutes. They indicate the extreme importance of chamber music in domestic life of the time. In this painting a viola da gamba is seen on the floor, available to play *basso continuo*[14] in an ensemble.

PLATE 30 (*facing page, above*)

Virginal by Hans Ruckers, Antwerp, 1598, compass GG/BB to c³ (collection of Madame la Comtesse de Chambure, Paris). Members of this Antwerp family made the finest harpsichords and virginals from about 1581 until 1680. Their instruments served as models for makers in France and England throughout the eighteenth century and are again being studied by twentieth-century builders. Paper on the virginal is block printed in the same design as that on the virginal in the Vermeer painting in plate 31.

PLATE 32

Double virginal by Hans Ruckers, Antwerp, late sixteenth century (Yale University Collection of Musical Instruments, Belle Skinner Collection, New Haven, Connecticut). The virginal at the left is tuned an octave higher (ie an *ottavino*) and can be played separately either in or out of the case or it can be removed and set above the other for playing both at once with the same set of jacks. The double virginal was a Flemish speciality. The Dutch musical-encyclopedist Reynvaan called it 'mother with child'.

PLATE 33
Double virginal by Hans
Ruckers the Elder, Ant-
werp, 1581 (Metropolitan
Museum of Art, New
York). This detail shows
the *ottavino* set above the
other keyboard as de-
scribed in the previous
caption.

PLATE 34

Claviorganum by Alexander Bortolotti, Venice, 1585 (Les Amis du Musée
Instrumental du Conservatoire Royal de Musique, Bruxelles). The
claviorganum is an instrument designed for versatility in which a harpsichord or virginal is combined with an organ. The two instruments can be
played separately or coupled together. At a later date some pianos were
'organized', the procedure for which was described by Bedos de Celles in
L'Art du facteur d'orgues, Paris, 1778.[15]

PLATE 35a and 35b

Painting and detail (*below*) by Friedrich von Falckenburg, Germany, 1619 (Germanisches Nationalmuseum, Nürnberg, Germany). This is the painted cover of the virginal that sat on top of an organ to make of it the claviorganum depicted in the picture. Only the cover now survives. The main portion of the painting shows the seasons in landscapes of the four estates of Lucas Friederich Behaim, who owned the instrument. Pictured in the center, a detail of which appears below, are musicians in the midst of autumnal wine-making festivities. They are playing the claviorganum which appears to have a small pedal board, two viole da gamba, a violin and a viola. Behaim himself is seen playing bass viola da gamba while the house music-master, Johann Staden, plays *basso continuo* on the claviorganum. The maker of the virginal, Paul Wissmayr, is standing to the right of the musicians together with the painter and Stefan Cuntz, the builder of the organ.

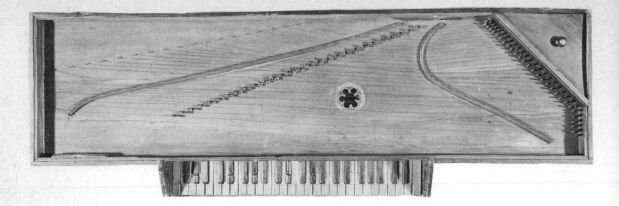

PLATE 36

Plan view of a virginal by Ionnes Battista Boni, Cortona, Italy, 1617; compass C/E to f³, 1 × 8′ (Smithsonian Institution, 60,1392, formerly Cooper Union Collection, New York). The system of tuning known as 'equal temperament' that came to be favored over others by the end of the eighteenth century and is now in general use divides the octave into twelve equal semi-tones permitting each accidental to serve for either a sharp or its nearest flat. One can then modulate freely from one key to another.

In other systems in use earlier a shade of difference exists between a sharp and the adjacent flat, and certain chromatic notes satisfactory in some keys are unworkable in others. The enharmonic keyboard shown here is for the purpose of producing this difference for some notes. It has accidentals divided from front to back for eb/d♯, g♯/ab, eb¹/d♯¹, g♯¹/ab¹. The front halves of the divided accidentals at the bottom extend the keyboard compass by short octave tuning as described on p31, while the back halves retain the F♯ and G♯ normally missing on short octave keyboards. This is known as 'broken octave' tuning. Many experiments were made with enharmonic compositions and keyboards divided into quarter-tones. Scipione Maffei included in his article of 1711 on Cristofori's piano (p52) a

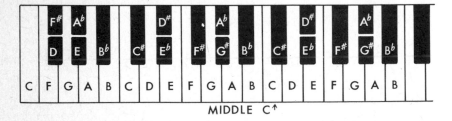

Fig. 3
Arrangement of keys of virginal above

description of a 'rare' harpsichord designed to cope with the problem of 'the tuning not being equal in all keys'. He saw it in Florence and described it as having five sets of keys one above the other tuned in such a manner that 'you may modulate and run through all the keys without any dissonance'. The Museo Civico in Bologna has such an instrument. At a later date some pianos were made with divided accidentals for 'unequal' tuning (see p68).

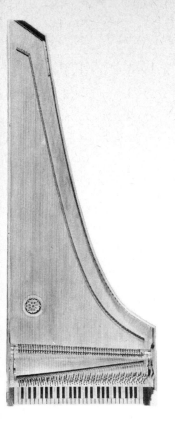

PLATE 37 (*left*)

Plan view of a harpsichord dated 1693 by an unknown Italian maker; compass GG to c³ (no GG♯), 1 × 8', two hand stops (Smithsonian Institution, 326,904, Hugo Worch Collection). The Italians were satisfied with a relatively simple harpsichord such as this throughout the Renaissance and Baroque eras. Two sets of 8' strings answered admirably their requirements which were mainly to accompany other instruments and/or voices. A typical Italian harpsichord of this date is lightly constructed and often provided with a heavier ornamented outer case. It was customary to remove the harpsichord from its case placing it on a table for performance.

The oldest extant harpsichord known was made in 1521 by Jerome of Bologna and is in the Victoria and Albert Museum, London.

PLATE 38

Spinet by Thomas Hitchcock, London, between 1703 and 1710; compass GG to g³, 1 × 8' (Smithsonian Institution, 62,382). This is still another form of the small domestic plucked-stringed keyboard instrument with one string for each key (see plates 27, 28, 29). The terminology for these instruments is confused, but several authorities have now agreed to use the term 'virginal' for the rectangular or polygonal instruments which have their keyboards and their strings parallel to the long sides, and 'spinet' for the small, bent side, wing-shaped instrument in which the tuning pins are in front above the keyboard and the strings are stretched diagonally.

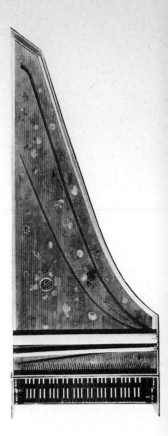

PLATE 39 (*above left*)

Harpsichord by Johannes Daniel Dulcken, Antwerp, 1745; compass FF to f³, 2 × 8′, 1 × 4′, lute, four hand stops (Smithsonian Institution, 315,758, Hugo Worch Collection). This beautiful instrument is in the fine tradition of harpsichord building established by the Ruckers family. It has two sets of strings at 8′ pitch, one playable from both keyboards, the other from the lower, one set of strings at 4′ pitch on the lower, and on the upper a 'lute' stop engaging a set of jacks which pluck close to the nut (ie the bridge on the wrest-plank) to produce a nasal lute-like sound.

    The earlier double harpsichords of the Flemings were usually, if not always, transposing instruments, the two manuals arranged so that they played at different pitches, usually a fourth or fifth apart. French seventeenth-century makers are associated with the development of the type of instrument shown here with two keyboards playing at the same pitch. Frank Hubbard calls them the 'expressive double'.[16]

PLATE 40 (*above right*)

Plan view of the harpsichord by Dulcken shown in the preceding plate. The Flemish and French harpsichord builders decorated the soundboards of their instruments with flowers, butterflies, etc, in delicate tempera colors in the charming manner shown here. The ornamental rosette set into a hole in this soundboard is a free design of gilt metal in which one would expect to find Dulcken's initials. They cannot, however, be clearly discerned, although the inclusion of the maker's initials was a Flemish guild

Fig. 4
Drawing of rose in soundboard of Dulcken harpsichord

regulation. The roses in Italian harpsichords or virginals are of abstract design and usually made of layers of parchment and gilded. Whatever their design or material, they have no function except as decoration or identification of the maker.

PLATE 41

Harpsichord made by Burkat Shudi in London, c. 1743; compass FF to f³ (no FF♯), 2 × 8', 1 × 4', lute, buff, five hand stops (Smithsonian Institution, 314,524, Hugo Worch Collection). This harpsichord is similar in its disposition to the one by Dulcken shown in Plate 39, ie two sets of 8' and one set of 4' strings, lute stop, and with an added stop (buff, sometimes called harp) which moves small leather pads against one set of 8' strings to produce a muted effect. The simple, handsome case of fine wood (here walnut burl veneer) with brass hardware is typical of the English makers.

Burkat Shudi (originally Burckardt Tschudi) was a Swiss who came to London as a joiner and soon thereafter became apprenticed to Hermann Tabel, a Fleming knowledgeable in the traditions of harpsichord building of his country. Shudi was making instruments under his own name by 1729. In 1761 he took as apprentice a young Scot, John Broadwood, who, eight years later, married Shudi's daughter. Ultimately the name of the firm changed to Shudi and Broadwood and the business continues to this day as the highly respected piano-making firm of John Broadwood and Sons, which is still operated by descendants of the founder.

PLATE 42

Burkat Shudi and his family, unknown painter, England, c. 1745 (copy) (collection of Captain Evelyn Broadwood, Capel, Surrey, England). The famous harpsichord-maker (1702–73) is shown here tuning his own instrument, his wife and two sons nearby. Shudi was prominent in London musical life. Handel frequented his house and possessed one of his harpsichords. The Mozarts, father and son, also knew him and admired his instruments. In 1766 he presented a two-manual harpsichord to Frederick the Great, who ordered two more and sent a ring to the maker.

PLATE 43

The Singing Party. Painting of the English school, mid-eighteenth century (National Gallery of Art, Washington, DC; gift of Duncan Phillips). Although painters rarely depicted men playing virginals, the artist here shows a man performing on a harpsichord that recalls the one by Shudi shown in plate 41. A typical eighteenth-century bassoon playing, it may be assumed, the bass line, while the keyboard plays the harmonic accompaniment from a figured bass.[17]

PLATE 44

Harpsichord by Benoist Stehlin, Paris, 1760; compass FF to f³, 2 × 8′, 1 × 4′, buff, shove coupler, two hand stops (Smithsonian Institution, 66,521). This is one of only two known surviving harpsichords by Benoist Stehlin, an emigrant from Switzerland to Paris. Like those by Dulcken (plate 39) and Shudi (plate 41), it has two sets of strings at 8′ pitch and one at 4′. The upper manual slides in to couple the two manuals, an arrangement known as 'shove coupler'.

The great names in French harpsichord-making were Pascal Taskin (1723–93) and the Blanchets: Nicholas (d. 1731), François Etienne (c. 1705–61) and François Etienne II (1730–66). Many Flemish harpsichords by members of the Ruckers family and others had been acquired by Frenchmen, and during the first half of the eighteenth century the French makers were adroit at extending their range up to five octaves to make them suitable for performing the music of Couperin, Rameau and others. Many of the Ruckers' instruments were altered in this way, an operation known as *ravalement*. The instruments built by the Blanchets and Taskin are modelled on these rebuilt instruments and are esteemed for their rich and brilliant tone.

Taskin is distinguished for having originated the *peau de buffle* stop—jacks with plectra made of buffalo hide producing sounds rhapsodically described in Diderot's *Encyclopedia* of 1788 as 'delicious and velvety . . . rich, mellow, suave and voluptuous'. He also invented knee levers to facilitate changes of registration.

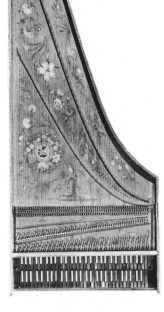

PLATE 45 (*above*)

Plan view of the harpsichord by Benoist Stehlin in the preceding plate. The rose contains the maker's initials and the date, 1760, is painted in red on the soundboard near the long side above and to the right of the rose.

43

PLATE 46

Mozart père et ses enfants. Watercolor by L. C. de Carmontelle, France, 1763 (Musée de Condé, Chantilly, France). The boy Mozart, aged seven, at a French harpsichord with his father and sister.

PLATE 47 (*facing page*)

Harpsichord by Hieronymus Hass, Hamburg, 1740; compass FF to f³ (no FF♯), three manuals, five sets of strings 1 × 16′, 2 × 8′, 1 × 4′ and 1 × 2′ (to c¹) (collection of Rafael Puyana, Paris). Although German writers have left us valuable treatises on the construction of musical instruments in the sixteenth and seventeenth centuries, surviving stringed keyboard instruments made in Germany before 1700 are scarce. The eighteenth-century clavichords and harpsichords are, however, among the finest. The Germans were especially fond of the clavichord and after rather primitive examples of the early eighteenth century more elaborate instruments made by fine craftsmen appeared. Far more clavichords than harpsichords are known; the former, much less expensive to make, was the keyboard instrument for most musical households and must have been quite prevalent. The clavichord by Voit made in 1812 (plate 18b) is evidence that the Germans were the last to give up the clavichord in favor of the piano.

The German harpsichords that have survived—some twenty-nine are at presently known—are unusually elegant and suitable for palaces, churches, theatres or opera houses. A great many must have been neglected or abandoned when the piano was finally accepted and old styles and practices gave way for the new.

The most prominent names among the eighteenth-century makers are

Hieronymus Albrecht Hass and his son Johann Adolph. They made no standard instrument and the various dispositions of their harpsichords indicate that each was made to order for its client. The use of 16' and 2' stops is extremely rare.

The one in this illustration is a *tour de force* and surely the *chef d'œuvre* of its maker. It might be said to possess an embarrassment of riches since the two-manual harpsichords shown in previous illustrations are fully adequate for the performance of the literature of the great harpsichord composers. The case is painted to simulate tortoise-shell and overlaid with Chinese scenes painted in gold. The picture inside the lid shows the harpsichord being presented to an unidentified lady. (Incidentally, this instrument is depicted on its own case, like the one in plates 35a and 35b.) The natural keys are covered with tortoise shell, the accidentals are ivory with tortoise shell inlay, and the keyboard surround is inlaid with these materials. If the bottom of the three keyboards is not to be used, it can be pushed into the instrument like the drawer of a chest.

PLATE 48

Plan view of the harpsichord by Hieronymus Hass in the preceding illustration.

PLATE 49

Harpsichord by Johann Adolf Hass, Hamburg, 1764; compass FF to f³, 2 × 8′, 1 × 4′ (Russell Collection, University of Edinburgh). Here is a simple but elegant harpsichord by the son of the maker of the unusually elaborate one in the two preceding plates. The beautiful case-work of mahogany veneer is applied even to the back (ie the long-side or spine). In general, this side, not intended to be seen, is left unfinished. The sound-board has no rose but is decorated with painted flowers. The instrument was restored about 1840 and it is possible that the present keyboard with ivory naturals and ebony accidentals replaced one with these materials reversed as was more usual in German instruments of this date. Documentary evidence indicates that this harpsichord once belonged to Mozart.

4

THE TRANSITION TO PIANO

By the beginning of the seventeenth century, musical trends had been set in motion which were to contribute ultimately to the invention of the piano and its acceptance as a replacement for the harpsichord.

The beginning of the period in music we now call Baroque is conveniently ascribed to the date 1600, and its end to the death of Johann Sebastian Bach in 1750, or, more precisely, that of George Frideric Handel nine years later.

Shortly before 1600 a group of Florentine musical intellectuals, known as the 'Camerata', discussed and speculated upon the nature of classical Greek drama, and specifically the style of musical utterance they believed to be its distinguishing characteristic.

The members of the Camerata voiced their dissatisfaction with the polyphonic music of the Renaissance with its thick layers of melodies interwoven and interdependent as an effective style for the expression of personal, subjective, dramatic and violent feelings. Not content merely to complain, several of their members wrote experimental operas. '*Daphne*' by Jacopo Peri, first performed in 1597, and his '*Euridice*', in 1600, are considered the first operas worthy of the name from both the musical and literary points of view. They introduce a new style of 'speech-song'—*stile rappresentivo* or *recitative*, ie a melody with a chordal accompaniment—a concept that was a total departure from polyphony.

The harmonic character of the chordal accompaniment brought with it awareness and appreciation of several tones heard simultaneously as a block of sound as opposed to the moving streams of individual melodies approaching, meeting and departing from each other point counter point. When the chordal accompaniment of the recitative acquired tonal centers, and points of repose were felt, music began to shift from modality towards tonality. Medieval folk singers had accompanied themselves with plucked strings, but it was during the Baroque era that the system of chordal progression that continues as a dominant force in the music of today was established. Two modes, major and minor, replaced the multiple ecclesiastical modes of former times, accomplishing the transition from mode to key which had begun to be felt in the late Renaissance.

Johann Sebastian Bach superbly realized in his music the fusion of the old and new styles, but even within his lifetime his music, the crowning glory of the Baroque, was considered out-moded. At his death in 1750 it was as though everything that could be said in the 'old style' had been said, so resolute was the turning away from it. Polyphony was to be no longer a way of musical life.

The harpsichord, as it had been in the Renaissance, continued to be in the Baroque the prevailing keyboard instrument of secular and non-liturgical music (the organ was then as now the basic keyboard instrument of the church). At first merely sharing a bass line played by a viola da gamba, cello or other low-voiced instrument, it supplied harmony that was indicated by figures appearing with the notes. (Indeed, the Baroque period is known as the 'age of the figured-bass' or *basso continuo*.)

Throughout the era individual instruments came into their own. No longer satisfied with leaving to the performers the choice of the instruments to play a composition, composers began to specify which ones were to be used and to write with awareness of the peculiar capabilities and limitations of the various families of instruments. Before the end of the Baroque they were writing idiomatically for individual instruments and the harpsichord assumed a more independent role and finally a 'life of its own'.

The vocal style inaugurated by opera was considered by some to be a bizarre innovation. Every trick of expression was tried: *crescendo* and *diminuendo* (not consciously employed earlier to any considerable extent), trills, vibrato, dynamic accents, even gasps and sobs, and other effects which can only be guessed at from texts of the time, in a determination to make the music convey the sense of words and express earthly and human, rather than lofty and abstract, emotions. These vocal practices had their effect on instrumental styles, and techniques of playing instruments underwent a gradual change. Roman orchestras, especially, began to attract attention to their experiments with a new style of dynamic expression and gradation.

The vast body of music of the period includes a glorious literature for solo keyboard instruments. In the Renaissance, organ and harpsichord or even lute and harpsichord had been used interchangeably. Only three or four examples of music printed before 1600 specify stringed keyboard instruments. Earliest among these is a group of pieces published in Venice by Antonio Gardane in 1551 for 'arpichordo, Clavicembalo, Spinette and Manicordi'.

The boastful claim of a work published in 1611 in England is therefore nearly justified: 'Parthenia or the Maydenhead of the first musicke that ever was printed for the Virginalls composed by three famous masters: William Byrd, Dr John Bull and Orlando Gibbons . . .' (The term virginal or virginals was used generically at this date for any member of the plucked-stringed keyboard family.) The pieces in this English collection were written in a manner eminently suitable to the instrument for which they were intended and the seventeenth century witnessed the development and flourishing of a truly harpsichordistic style.

The Elizabethan composers and their followers produced a cherished treasury of harpsichord music before the center of this activity shifted to the continent. There its climax was achieved in the works of Louis and François Couperin, Jean-Phillippe Rameau, Johann Sebastian Bach, George Frideric Handel, Domenico Scarlatti and numerous others. It cannot be charged that the music of these great composers strained the resources of the harpsichord, and yet François Couperin seemed to express a hint of apology for it when in 1713 in the introduction to his first book of harpsichord pieces he wrote: 'The harpsichord is perfect in its compass and brilliant in itself; but as one cannot increase or diminish its sounds, I will be forever grateful to those who by an infinite art supported by taste will succeed in rendering this instrument capable of expression.'

In his *L'art de toucher le clavecin*, published in 1717, Couperin set forth his ideas of performance. These were aimed at achieving greater emotional and sensitive expression and the full realization of the harpsichord's capabilities —an indication that he was advocating improvement in performance rather than changes in the instrument itself.

Nevertheless, the expressive vocal and instrumental style that had been developing for more than 100 years was threatening the harpsichord with obsolescence since *crescendo*, *diminuendo*, and dynamic accents by means of touch were beyond its scope. A keyboard instrument combining the expressive potential of the clavichord with the sonority of the harpsichord now seemed called for. The moment was ripe for the appearance of the piano. Unknown to Couperin in 1713, it had, in fact, been invented some years earlier in Florence, but it was not to rival seriously the harpsichord for some sixty years.

PLATE 50 (*next page*)

Harpsichord by Burkat Shudi and Johannes Broadwood, London, 1773. Compass CC to f³, 2 × 8', 1 × 4', lute, buff, machine, Venetian swell, six handstops, two pedals (Les Amis du Musée Instrumental du Conservatoire Royal de Musique, Bruxelles). This harpsichord was a gift from King Frederick the Great to Empress Maria Theresa. Joseph Haydn acquired a similar one from Shudi's workshop after the maker's death. Fine as it is, it represents a phase of the decline of the harpsichord and an attempt to compete with the piano, the popularity of which was, by this date a threat. It contains devices to produce effects intended to compensate for the 'limitations' of the instrument, these limitations being in fact the true nature of the harpsichord. One is the 'Venetian swell' invented by Shudi in 1769 and consisting of louvers which can be opened and closed by the pedal on the right to achieve *crescendo* and *diminuendo*. Another addition is a machine stop for quick changes of registration, operated by the left pedal. In the most idiomatic of music for the harpsichord, however, *crescendo* and *diminuendo* effects are achieved by the addition or subtraction of notes to thicken or thin the musical texture and changes of registration are adequate between

sections or at pauses or breaks where enough time is allowed by the structure of the music.

The Venetian swell is not successful on the harpsichord; open or closed it muffles the sound when it is placed over the soundboard. Nevertheless, it was successfully adopted for organs and was sometimes applied to early pianos including the upright by John Isaac Hawkins in plate 86, and also a square (c. 1790) by Charles Albrecht of Philadelphia, both in the Hugo Worch Collection, Smithsonian Institution.

Another attempt to produce gradation of volume was made as early as 1754 by Jacob Kirckman in England with a device known as 'nag's head swell' in which a hinged portion of the lid is raised and lowered by a pedal. Since it can be operated only when the lid is closed, it, too, is ineffective musically. It is, however, quite comical visually; when the flap of the lid opens and closes the harpsichord suggests some curious monster gasping for air. The idea was used by Erard in the piano shown in plate 63.

5

PIANOS

EARLY EXPERIMENTS

Some experiments with new types of keyboard instruments were made early in the Baroque era. Two instruments called *piano e forte* were mentioned in letters to the Duke of Modena in 1598. Provocative though the name is and tempting as it is to imagine them to be early pianos, no description exists. In 1600 Hans Haydn of Nürnberg attempted a mechanism for bowing the strings of a harpsichord for an additional effect; a Dutch instrument of 1610 having hammers attached to keys but without dampers is said to have been known at one time in a Paris collection; Marin Mersenne, in his treatise of 1636, *Harmonie Universelle*, showed a xylophone with keys, the ends of which struck the bars of wood from below.

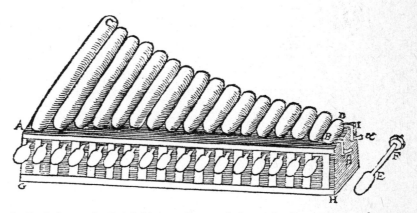

Fig. 5
Mersenne's keyed xylophone

In Paris in 1708, Cuisinié experimented along the line of Haydn's earlier attempt to make a more expressive keyboard instrument. A treadle-operated resined wheel was attached to an instrument whose strings were struck by tangents similar to those of a clavichord; both hands of the performer were free to play on the keyboard while the resined wheel bowed the strings much in the manner of a hurdy-gurdy. These and other similar isolated ventures, however, had no perceptible influence on the evolution of the piano.

BARTOLOMEO CRISTOFORI AND THE FLORENTINE PIANO

Sometime before 1700, Bartolomeo Cristofori, a harpsichord-maker in charge of the musical instrument collection of Prince Ferdinand dei Medici in Florence, replaced harpsichord jacks with leather topped hammers activated by a remarkable mechanical system. The result was an instrument

51

capable of being played loud or soft, of making dynamic accents, and of producing gradations of sound. Not quite aware that he had invented a new instrument, the maker called it *gravicembalo col piano e forte*—harpsichord with soft and loud.

Apart from the hammers, the most striking differences between Cristofori's *gravicembalo col piano e forte* and the other struck-stringed keyboard instrument then in use, the clavichord, were the substitution of hammers covered with leather for metal tangents, a wing-shaped rather than a rectangular instrument, a synchronized damper system, and, most important, an action introducing an 'escapement'. The last feature is essential to a completely successful piano.

The mechanism or the 'action' of a piano involves the tossing of a hammer against a string or several strings tuned in unison. Once the hammer has struck it must immediately fall back from the strings so that they may continue vibrating—a process contrived by a system of levers. Dynamic control is aided by an arrangement that causes the final toss of the hammer to take place from a point quite close to the strings just at the instant the key is fully depressed. The hammer then drops back farther than the distance of this final leap in order to be ready to play again. The mechanism that controls the hammer's upward course and its rebound is known as 'escapement'.

Further refinements are a back-check and a synchronized damper system. The back-check cushions the rebound of the hammer to prevent its bouncing up again from the excess energy of the stroke on the key and bobbing against the strings causing a loss of tone.

In the damper system each key has its own damper that sits on the strings until the hammer strikes them and lifts off at that instant, leaving the strings free to vibrate as long as the key is held down. When the key is released the damper returns to its place.

Cristofori's remarkable invention is the basis of the action of present-day pianos. More than 100 years were to elapse before it was significantly improved.

His first back-check is a pair of crossed threads that cradles the hammer as it falls, but his later version is an upright of wood covered with a soft material that provides enough friction to discourage the hammer's undesirable return. This latter device is still in use.

In 1711 an Italian intellectual, Scipione Maffei, published an article reporting that he had seen four of the new pianos.[18] The date 1709 usually given for the invention of the piano seems to have been based on the year of Maffei's visit to the maker's workshop. We know now, however, that the invention was accomplished sometime between 1693 (when Cristofori was summoned by the prince to Florence from his native Padua) and the year 1700.[19]

Cristofori made some changes between his earliest pianos and the improved model of 1726 (plate 51), but the basic principle of the mechanism may be understood from the following sketch and explanation included in Maffei's enthusiastic article.[20]

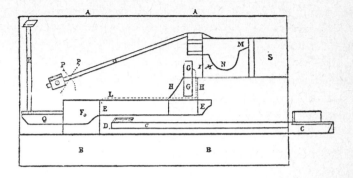

Fig. 6
Cristofori piano action

A String
B Frame of the keyboard
C The key or first lever, which at its extremity raises the second lever
D The block on the first lever by which it acts
E The second-lever, on each side of which is a jawbone-shaped piece to support the little tongue or hopper
F The pivot of the second lever
G The movable tongue (hopper), which, being raised by the second lever (E), forces the hammer upwards
H The jawbone-shaped pieces between which the hopper is pivoted
I The strong brass wire pressed together at the top, which keeps the hopper in its place
L The spring of brass wire that goes under the hopper and holds it pressed firmly against the wire which is behind it
M The receiver in which all the butts of the hammers rest
N The circular part of the hammers, which rests in the receiver
O The hammer, which, when pressed upwards by the hopper, strikes the string with the leather on its top
P The strings of silk, crossed, on which the stems, or shanks, of the hammers rest
Q The end of the second lever (E), which becomes lowered by the act of striking the key
R The dampers, which are lowered when the key is touched, leaving the string free to vibrate, and stop the sound on returning to their places
S Part of the frame to strengthen the receiver

Cristofori's piano seems to have attracted little general attention in Italy in his lifetime, but a year after his death in 1731 a set of sonatas was written for it and published in Florence. A manuscript is preserved at the British Museum. Dynamic changes are significantly indicated in the score by the terms *forte*, *piano*, *piu piano* and in one instance *piu forte*. These compositions are the earliest published music for piano. The title page reads (in translation):

Sonatas
for harpsichord with soft and loud commonly called
with small hammers
dedicated
to His Royal Highness
the Most Serene Prince D. Antonio
of Portugal
and composed
by D. Lodovico Giustini di Pistoia
first work
Florence 1732

The dedication is to the son of the King of Portugal. Both Prince Antonio and his sister Princess Maria Barbara were lovers of music and were devoted pupils of Domenico Scarlatti, who accompanied the princess to the Spanish court when she married the Spanish king in 1729.

Perhaps the prince played the Giustini sonatas on the Florentine pianos, but Scarlatti took little interest in pianos (although there are said to have been five of them in the Spanish court at one time[21]) and continued to compose his incomparable sonatas for harpsichord.

Cristofori's few pupils went their separate ways at his death; at least one may have found his way to Dresden to influence the beginnings of piano-making there. Another, Giovanni Ferrini, made the piano that was used at the Spanish court in Scarlatti's time by the famous *castrato* singer, Farinelli.

GOTTFRIED SILBERMANN AND THE PIANO

It often happens that when the time is ripe several people conceive the same idea at about the same time—so it was with the invention of the piano. It was, to borrow a phrase from Victor Hugo, 'an idea whose time had come'.

One stimulus was the remarkable playing of an oversized dulcimer by one Pantaleon Hebenstreit. Hebenstreit's gargantuan hammered dulcimer was more than 9ft long—twice the size of those in general use—and had two soundboards, one strung with over-spun catgut, the other with wire strings, some 185 in all.

He played it with stunning virtuosity using double-faced hammers, one side of hard, the other of soft leather. His performances were admired as early as 1697, and when he played for Louis XIV he was honored by the king's proposal that his instrument be called the 'pantaleon'. It allowed for great contrast in dynamics and variety of tone color, but its popularity with other performers was limited due to the extreme difficulty of playing and maintaining it.

Hebenstreit's appearance in Paris in 1705 possibly gave Jean Marius the ideas for four models of '*clavecins à maillets*'—harpsichords with mallets—two of which had down-striking actions: mechanized pantaleons, as it were. These were crude in comparison to the Cristofori instruments and they had no dampers or provision for escapement. Marius showed them at the Royal Academy of Sciences of Paris in 1716, but if the ideas were ever transformed into instruments, which is doubtful, they were quickly forgotten.

In 1714 Hebenstreit became pantaleonist in the court orchestra at Dresden, and in 1717 Christoph Gottlieb Schröter, an organist, writer and instrument maker, after hearing him there, devised two piano actions, one up-striking and one down-striking. Yet in spite of his claim to have invented the piano in Germany, there is no evidence that he succeeded in incorporating his ideas in a musical instrument.

Gottfried Silbermann, a great German organ-builder, was, however, more persistent. He, too, had admired Hebenstreit's playing, and had begun making pantaleons until restrained by an edict prohibiting imitations of the original. Meanwhile, Maffei's article on the Cristofori piano had been translated into German. Probably this translation, along with his experiences with pantaleons, inspired Silbermann to make two pianos which he showed to Johann Sebastian Bach in 1736. Bach admired the tone but complained that the action was heavy and the upper register weak. Silbermann was discouraged, yet his interest did not flag and he continued working on his pianos. After ten more years, during which he very possibly saw a Cristofori instrument, courage again in hand, he brought one of them to the attention of King Frederick II of Prussia (later known as Frederick the Great). The king was delighted and some accounts say he acquired fifteen Silbermann pianos. Only three, however, have survived into this century (plate 53).

The next year Bach went to Potsdam to visit his son, Carl Phillip Emmanuel, chamber-musician to King Frederick since 1740. The older Bach was invited to the palace and led around the various rooms to try the pianos. Whether he was genuinely enthusiastic or merely deferential to royalty is difficult to tell from contemporary accounts, but he was more favorably impressed this time and he obligingly improvised a fugue on a subject supplied by the king. There was little opportunity in the three years left to him to indulge in experimentation with a new instrument, but the event is immortalized in his final great work, *The Musical Offering*, developed from King Frederick's theme. Silbermann is credited, with the inauguration of piano-making in Germany, and for a time it was believed by some in that country that he was the inventor of the piano.

THE TWILIGHT ERA

In the 'twilight zone' between rejection of the harpsichord and full acceptance of the piano many experiments were tried in an effort to prolong the
life of the harpsichord (see plate 50). Conversely, early piano-makers, as
though loath to abandon the harpsichord once and for all, added stops
which lowered strips of metal, leather, or cloth on to the strings to suggest
a harpsichord sound. One of the Silbermann pianos in the palace at Potsdam
has a *cembalo* stop, indication of frank nostalgia.

In the last years of the eighteenth century, some makers were producing
harpsichords and pianos in the same workshop. One of these was Pascal
Taskin, a great French maker (see page 43) (plate 62). A few instruments
were made combining the two with one manual for the harpsichord and a
second for the piano, or with a set of hammers superimposed on the
harpsichord action and put into operation by means of a pedal.

Several composers including C. P. E. Bach and Jacob Kirkman of the
harpsichord-making family wrote compositions for two performers—one
playing harpsichord and the other the piano—a medium possible only on
the early pianos with a light tone that does not overpower the harpsichord.
These compositions were scarcely more successful than the combination
instruments.

There was, naturally, some resistance to change. No doubt many agreed
with Voltaire when in 1774 he called the piano, compared with the harpsichord, 'a boiler-maker's instrument'. But Charles Burney, the English
music-historian, having described pianos and improvements in their
mechanisms, said that 'the harsh scratching [!] of the quills of a harpsichord can now no longer be borne'.[22]

Some musical families acquired the 'new-fangled' instruments without
discarding their cherished harpsichords. An inventory made by the
Commission Temporaire des Arts of instruments confiscated during the
French Revolution listed sixty-two harpsichords and spinets, 'the rarest
in their perfection', designated (though few reached their destination) to
be sent to the Conservatory 'to serve as models because of their working
principles'. Twenty-five of the houses where these were found also contained pianos.

Well before the end of the eighteenth century, however, the musical
world had begun to recognize that the piano was here to stay, and that it
was not simply an 'improved' harpsichord or clavichord, but a different
instrument that required a new style of composition. Some consider the
three sonatas composed in 1773 by Muzio Clementi, the famous pianist
and enterprising London publisher and dealer in musical instruments, to
be the first music in a style completely suited to piano. These sonatas

established the form of the classical piano sonata. Mozart and Haydn were quick to meet the challenge and others followed suit.

Meanwhile, economic and social factors influenced the increased use of the piano. Clavichords were inexpensive but their uses were limited. Harpsichords cost more than the early pianos and, requiring frequent requilling, were more difficult to maintain. The material resources of the rising middle class encouraged musical amateurs and created a climate favorable to the new keyboard instrument.

Mozart's mother had written to her husband from Mannheim in 1777: 'Everyone thinks the world of Wolfgang here, but indeed he plays quite differently from what he used to in Salzburg [plate 46]—for there are pianofortes here, on which he plays so extraordinarily well that people say they have never heard the like.'[23] Mozart's own important keyboard compositions, except for the early concerto arrangements of works by other composers, are for piano and were written in true pianistic style like those of Haydn. After 1777 Mozart turned more and more to the piano. In plate 60, a painting of 1781 preserved in the Mozart residence in Salzburg, he is seen playing piano duets with his sister—doubtless one of the four-hand compositions for piano that he wrote in the 1780s.

Joseph Haydn had virtually abandoned the harpsichord in favor of the piano some time before 1790. In a letter of February of this year, melancholy upon returning from Vienna to Esterháza, he wrote to his cherished friend, Marianne von Genzinger: 'Nothing could console me; my whole lodging was in disorder; my piano that I usually love in other times was moody and disobedient and provoked my displeasure more than it consoled me.'[24] Not a word about his harpsichord! (Among his instruments were the two-manual harpsichord by Shudi and Broadwood mentioned earlier and a Viennese piano made by J. Wenzel Schanz.) In the same year he advised a friend to give away his harpsichord and buy a piano.

JOHANNES ZUMPE AND THE ENGLISH PIANO

Experimentation, invention, and rivalry were lively among piano-makers once a workable instrument had been developed in Germany. England lagged behind until 1760 but in this year twelve piano-craftsmen arrived in England bringing with them traditions owed to both Silbermann and Cristofori. Some of them came from Gottfried Silbermann's workshop, their craft having been disrupted by the Seven Years' War. Johannes Zumpe, one pupil of Silbermann, had the good fortune to be taken into Burkat Shudi's harpsichord workshop (plates 41, 42), as did a young man coming from Scotland the following year, John Broadwood (plate 50). The history of piano-making owes much to these men.

Zumpe developed a piano action which was a simplification of the Cristo-fori-Silbermann ideas and, returning to the clavichord shape, installed it in an oblong horizontal case. This instrument unaccountably came to be known as a 'square' piano (plate 55).

The arrival of Johann Christian Bach in London in 1762 was auspicious for both Zumpe and the future of the piano. This youngest son of Johann Sebastian came to prefer the piano over the harpsichord and in 1768 gave the first solo piano performance in an English concert using a Zumpe square.

For reasons unknown—perhaps as an economy measure—Zumpe omitted in his pianos the escapement and the check so cleverly worked out by his predecessors. Despite this obvious disadvantage, his little compact economical pianos soon acquired a great vogue not only in England but on the continent as well. They could scarcely be made fast enough to supply the demand and their maker prospered. Before long, square pianos became so widespread that it is said they were found even in the harems of Middle Eastern countries; they were supposed to be equipped with short legs so that the performer could be seated on cushions on the floor. In a painting of an English family in their Florentine villa between 1772 and 1776, it is not surprising, therefore, to see them making music with what is, almost certainly, a Zumpe piano[25] brought with them from home (plate 56).

The Zumpe mechanism came to be known as the 'English single action'. Later John Geib, a German working for Longman and Broderip in London, added an escapement and patented his 'English double action' in 1786 which was used in more expensive square pianos. The so-called English action is, in fact, international in its development. Invented in Italy by Cristofori, carried on in Germany by Silbermann, adapted to English needs by Zumpe, a German, it was refined and developed by another German, John Geib. It eventually emerged as the successful English grand action first made by John Broadwood, a Scot, who gave much of the credit for its success to Robert Stodart, an Englishman, and Americus Backers from Holland.

JOHANN ANDREAS STEIN AND THE GERMAN PIANO

In October of 1777 Mozart, in a letter to his father from Augsburg, mentioned the pianos of Johann Stein:

> This time I shall begin at once with Stein's pianos. Before I had seen any of his make, Späth's claviers had always been my favourites.[26] But now I much prefer Stein's for they damp ever so much better than the Regensburg instruments. When I strike hard, I can keep my finger on the note or raise it, but the sound ceases the moment I have produced it. In whatever way I touch the keys, the tone is always even. It never jars, it is never stronger or weaker or entirely absent; in a word it is always even. . .His instruments have this special advantage over others that they are made with escape action. Only one maker in a hundred bothers about this. But without an escapement it is impossible to avoid jangling and vibration after the note is struck. When you touch the keys, the hammers fall back again the moment after they have struck the strings, whether you hold down the keys or release them[27] [plate 57].

Stein had learned organ-building in Strasbourg from Johann Andreas Silbermann, a nephew of the famous Gottfried. When he began piano-making sometime after settling in Augsburg in 1750, he experimented not with the Gottfried Silbermann type of pianos but with the kind of action developed quite independently by a group of Bavarian makers who were apparently aiming at an improved clavichord. Their first efforts were crude (plate 54), but the idea eventually produced a fine piano accepted by Mozart, Haydn, Beethoven and others. These craftsmen—no single name stands out among them—had developed a Prellemechanik, which Stein improved by adding an escapement. Although Gottfried Silbermann built the first successful piano in Germany, it was the Stein action which came to be known as 'German'. Later it was called 'Viennese' after Stein's son, Mathaus, and daughter, Nannette, moved to Vienna and carried on the business there. Brother and sister worked together at first then separated to found independent firms. Nannette (Stein) Streicher (she had married Johann Streicher before leaving Augsburg) became the first and only woman to attain prominence in the piano industry. She is also remembered for her devoted and protective friendship for Beethoven—a relationship that had among its rewards the benefit of many conversations on piano construction from the point of view of the composer and performer.

For a century the Viennese and English actions both enjoyed favor. Some preferred the light touch and tone of the former, others the more resistant touch and powerful tone of the latter. Many makers produced both types in their workshops to cater for the inclinations of their clients. The last pianos with Viennese action were made during the opening years of the twentieth century. The modern piano is based on the Cristofori-Silbermann-English principles and certain refinements added to it have produced a piano with a degree of the touch-sensitive quality claimed for the Viennese action (plates 58, 59).

POSSIBILITIES AND PROBLEMS

As the possibilities of the piano were realized, composers and performers made more and more demands of it. Program or descriptive music became the rage in the late eighteenth century. This was no new idea—the biblical sonatas of Johann Kuhnau and the harpsichord pieces of Rameau and Couperin with descriptive titles such as *La Poule (The Hen)* and *Le Rappel des Oiseaux (The Call of the Birds)* were not isolated examples—but a taste indulged by some early nineteenth-century composers to imitate booming canons, thunder, the sound of waves, and other natural phenomena were bound to strain the resources of the piano.

The problem of sustaining a note also became a matter of concern. Clavichord performers had been able to accomplish this with some success by the use of vibrato (*Bebung*), and harpsichord composers had ornamented with trills and turns a note to be prolonged. Pianists continued the practice of ornamentation and also adopted the expedient of fast repetition of a note to carry over its sound. Earlier piano actions could not articulate adequately for these performance devices.

Other problems plagued makers. Greater volume was not only desired by composers and performers for expressing more powerful, dramatic, *fortissimo* writing, but needed, too, for larger concert halls and orchestras. To meet this demand string tension was increased, necessitating heavier stringing and placing greater stress on the frame of the piano. Additional stress was created by the increasing keyboard compass, pushing up to $7\frac{1}{4}$ octaves (AAA to c^5) before the end of the nineteenth century, and by the elevation of pitch. This rose from as low as 415 cycles to the second for a^1 to 421.6 in Mozart's time and as high as 456 later in Vienna before 440 was established by the International Standards Association in 1939.[28] Experiments which continue unceasingly today were constantly being tried to produce a piano with a more resonant and more beautiful tone, an action responsive and dependable under all conditions, and tuning and mechanism that remain stable in atmospheric changes.

These qualities are determined in a number of ways: the degree of communication between the strings and the soundboard accomplished by the strings constantly pressing the bridge firm against the soundboard that is forced up by the framing (ie crowned) into a slightly convex shape; the resonant capacity of the soundboard; the nature of the material of the strings and of the covering of the hammers; the arrangement and the determination of the gauges of the strings; the point at which the hammer strikes the strings; a hammer action capable of reacting to a powerful stroke or to a light delicate touch and of restriking a note with great rapidity; control of extreme changes in the various materials due to fluctuations of temperature and humidity.

Every aspect of the construction of the piano has come under critical scrutiny: the action has constantly been re-studied for means of improvement; for the soundboard many kinds of wood and seasoning have been tried as well as variations in the thickness and in the direction of the grain of the wood; the thin leather covering of the hammers was supplemented by cloth under the leather, and a variety of other materials were tried before the shaped layers of felt used today were adopted; experiments were made in covering the steel strings with copper or silver for greater elasticity, and in the manner of securing them at both ends; and a faster-acting and more responsive damper pedal was developed.

Along with efforts to improve and refine piano action and tone a remarkable assortment of cabinet styles were designed (plates 66, 68, 73, 74, 75, 80) small and large uprights as well. While new styles of piano composition were being created and performance techniques developed, the piano became more important to family and social life (plates 64, 65, 72, 81, 82).

Even before the end of the eighteenth century the piano—no longer the exclusive property of kings and noblemen—began to be found in the homes of the rising middle class. Once Zumpe had shown the practicality and saleability of a piano more economical to make and easier to accommodate in a modest setting, others began to occupy themselves with new sizes and shapes. Early experiments had been made to develop a vertical instrument (plate 66) before William Stodart of London, looking back to the clavicytherium (plate 26) brought out in 1795 his 'upright grand'—a small grand up-ended, installed in a rectangular case and set on a stand (plate 68). This was more successful than previous attempts at a vertical piano and others followed his example.

Pianos were sometimes provided with pedal boards on which the lowest notes could be played (plate 61). Earlier some clavichords, harpsichords and virginals were so equipped (plates 35a and 35b). These were intended primarily for organ practice.

Between 1716 and 1851 an astonishing number of patents[29] were registered for ideas dealing with every aspect of the craft. Some never got beyond the drawing board; others were tried and abandoned and still others were refined, developed and adopted as standard. The history of the piano through the nineteenth century is opaque with the multiplicity and complexity of experiments and inventions.

SÉBASTIEN ERARD AND THE FRENCH PIANO

The earliest successful piano-maker in France was Sébastien Erard who came to Paris from Alsace in 1768 and worked first as apprentice to a harpsichord-maker. He made his first piano in 1777. It was probably the first one made in France and was a square model containing the English type of action probably patterned after the pianos of Johanne Zumpe which were already popular in France (plate 63).

The enterprising Sébastien opened a workshop in London while his brother carried on the business in Paris, and the acquisition of one of their pianos by the First Consul, Napoleon Bonaparte, brought them deserved attention.

Through the succeeding decades the Erards made many contributions to the improvement of the piano, the most important of which is the repetition action developed by Sébastien and patented by his nephew in 1821. Sébastien was familiar with both the English grand action and the Viennese action and achieved a combination of the best qualities of each: the stability and solidity of the former and the sensitive responsiveness of the latter. The repetition or double escapement mechanism is a complicated system of springs and levers which arrest the hammer in its rebound after it has struck the strings. The practical result is that as long as the key is held down the hammer remains close to the strings instead of returning to its original position so that if a note is to be repeated the hammer has a much shorter distance to travel in order to strike the strings again. Its advantage to the performer is obvious: a succession of repeated notes can be executed with greater ease and speed, and dynamic shadings can be more delicately controlled.

The action involved such an intricate assemblage of moving parts that the first examples of it easily went out of order. Moreover the mechanism was noisy. But Erard continued to work on it and Henri Herz, a pianist and inventor, simplified and refined it. The Herz-Erard action met with the full approval of performers and modern action incorporates its principles.

Two other improvements by the Erards were widely adopted: the agraffe—a metal stud pierced with a hold for each string to pass through—invented in 1806 by Sébastien and the harmonic bar, devised by Pierre in 1838. Both of these are for the dual purpose of precisely fixing the down-bearing of the bridge to ensure communication between the bridge and soundboard and to prevent the hammers from dislodging the strings from their proper place on the bridge.

Sébastien Erard is also responsible for a revolutionary improvement in the harp—an arrangement of pedals known as double action making it possible to play in all keys, and which is applied to modern harps.

PIANISTS AND PIANOS

The nineteenth century saw the development of virtuoso piano technique, and piano-makers were hard pressed to meet the demands of pianists like Franz Liszt and Frédéric Chopin.

Liszt with his dazzling heroic style (plates 76, 77) seems to have played any and all pianos in his vigorous concert career; Chopin's expressive style, distinguished by extraordinary delicacy and subtlety of nuance, seems to have been best accommodated by the French pianos of Pleyel (plate 78) and Erard. Liszt said, 'Chopin was fond of Pleyel pianos because of their silvery and somewhat veiled sonority and their easy touch',[30] and Chopin said, 'When I am in a bad mood, I play Erard pianos and easily find in them a ready-made sound. But when I am in good spirits and strong enough to find the sounds I want I use Pleyel pianos.'[31] In 1848 he wrote from London that he had three pianos in his rooms, an Erard, a Pleyel and a Broadwood. In England he customarily played a Broadwood in concert.

John Field and Chopin share credit for the inauguration of a virtuoso pedal technique that increases sustaining power, enhances singing tone, and can even, in a mysterious way, produce a silhouette of a note or line against a background of diffused harmonies, a technique carried to its ultimate in the evanescent magical effects of the impressionistic music of Claude Debussy and Maurice Ravel.

A well-known painting of Franz Liszt surrounded by adoring listeners (plate 76) gives an excellent impression of his romantic aura. More than any other single performer, he raised the status of the performing musician from that of servant to the rich, to one of respect, adulation and glamour. His pianistic virtuosity greatly influenced piano-making. Using the full weight and strength of shoulders, arms and wrists he made the instrument speak with a power, drama, and even violence that it had never done before. His style of playing, as well as his compositions, represent the essence of the Romantic movement. Pianos suffered at his hands and it was not at all unusual for one or more strings to break and for the piano to require re-tuning in the midst of one of his concerts. In fact, on occasions a spare piano stood ready on the stage and reports of his concerts suggest that the audience felt cheated if a piano survived intact (plate 77). He played the finest available European pianos and on at least one occasion an American Chickering. In his Weimar studio Liszt had a Steinway concert grand.

Piano-playing by women in the nineteenth century was considered an attractive social accomplishment (plate 81) much as playing the virginal was two centuries earlier (plate 31). Some women were serious and highly accomplished pianists, but few followed the example of Clara Schumann (plate 79), daughter of a fine pianist and teacher, wife of Robert Schumann, confidante of Johannes Brahms and the first to play many of his works. Her professional concert career gave courage and inspiration to others of her sex.

Another composer who influenced the development of the piano in the nineteenth century was Beethoven, who often wanted it to sound like an orchestra. In 1818 he received a grand piano as a gift from the Broadwood firm (plate 71), his first six-octave instrument; his last three monumental sonatas were composed after he became its proud owner. His keyboard compositions until the third concerto, published in 1804, were contained within a five-octave compass as were all of Mozart's and most of Haydn's. Erard had presented him with a piano of five and a half octaves (FF to c^4) in 1803 (plate 70).

Beethoven's experiences with pianos were not always happy. The following account by a professor at the Paris Conservatory of a performance by Beethoven that probably took place some time between 1803 and 1808 is vivid evidence that the piano provided at the time was not, to put it mildly, equal to the occasion:

> One evening when Beethoven was playing a Mozart piano concerto . . . he asked me to turn the pages for him. But I was mostly occupied in wrenching out the strings of the piano which snapped, while the hammers stuck among the broken strings. Beethoven insisted upon finishing the concerto, so back and forth I leaped jerking out a string, disentangling a hammer, turning a page, and I worked harder than Beethoven.[32]

Difficulties of a similar nature were plaguing other pianists. Carl Maria von Weber in an unfinished novel describes a scene (perhaps autobiographical) in which the overwrought hero strikes a low C on the piano: 'The hammer flew out of its fork and a number of strings gave up their lives crunchingly—thus did the anger that so violently overwhelmed me dash my hand upon the keys. . . .'[33]

Beethoven wrote to thank the Broadwoods effusively for their gift even before their piano arrived, but once he tried it it can only have been the feel of the heavier action and the extended keyboard compass that gave him pleasure rather than the sound, for in 1818 his deafness, as early as 1798 a matter of extreme anxiety, had progressed to the point that he probably could not judge the quality of the tone. Desperately frustrated, he appealed often to his friends, the Streichers, to adjust his Broadwood or provide another piano audible to him, and he did not wholly abandon the Viennese instruments. In the last years of his life the well-known Viennese maker, Conrad Graf, put at his disposal one of his quadruple-strung pianos in the vain hope that it would be audible to him. It had four strings to a note except for the lowest bass notes and was an attempt to produce greater sonority, not successfully accomplished until the adoption later of the iron frame.

The Beethoven Broadwood contains the English grand action developed by several makers on the basis of Cristofori and Silbermann ideas and first made by the Broadwoods. It was in a sense a 'pushing' rather than a 'bouncing' action; it was heavier, required more muscle power and produced greater volume of tone than the Viennese action. The pedals replacing the hand-stops and knee-levers of earlier instruments were a Broadwood innovation dating from 1783.

Although some of Beethoven's compositions were published until 1802 with titles designating them for harpsichord or piano, it is unlikely that he ever played them on a harpsichord or encouraged anyone else to do so. It is doubtful, in fact, whether he used harpsichord to any great extent after 1782 when, at the age of twelve in Bonn, he played continuo under the direction of his teacher, Cristian Gottlob Neefe, in the orchestra of the Court Theatre of Elector Max Friederich.

Publishers had to sell their music, and the 'harpsichord' on the title page encouraged purchase by those who had not yet acquired pianos to replace the older and increasingly obsolete instruments. This wording, however, disappears from the title pages of most music about 1800, in line with the virtual suspension of harpsichord-making.

The social status attached to the possession of a Broadwood grand piano in the nineteenth century is suggested by a painting of 1824 (page 65) of a family in India. On the left is a Broadwood grand—obviously a prized possession. A Broadwood grand was so important to at least one Englishman serving his country in India that it was worth the expense of transporting it there and the considerable trouble of keeping it in playing condition to help create a corner of England in an out-post of empire.

Ignaz Pleyel, the founder of the great French firm bearing his name was born in Austria, became a musical child prodigy, studied with Joseph Haydn before serving for a time at the Court of Naples, was for ten years chapel-master of Strasbourg Cathedral, appeared in concerts, and after reprieve from a death sentence during the Revolution, established his residence in Paris in the early years of the nineteenth century. Putting his musical background to good use, he first went into music publishing. Then in 1807, at the age of fifty, he started a piano factory that he operated for seventeen years before turning it over to his son, Camille. Although talented as a composer and pianist, Camille chose to devote himself to piano-making and seriously applied himself to studying the craft in London with Broadwood, Collard and Clementi. Camille was intimate with the great figures of the piano world, including Chopin. Salle Pleyel, which he built in Paris about 1829, has been and continues to be the scene of many historic concerts by Chopin, Anton Rubinstein, Kalkbrenner, Hummel, Saint-Saëns and their successors. The firm name changed several times to include new partners, in 1887 becoming Pleyel, Lyon and Company under the guidance of Gustave Lyon.

That Henri Matisse incorporated the name Pleyel in his painting *The Piano Lesson*—a unique use of a piano trade name—suggests the degree to which the name is a household word in France. By the beginning of the twentieth century 'Pleyel', along with 'Bechstein' in Germany and 'Broadwood' in England, was virtually a synonym for piano.

Yet the craft was not entirely dominated by European firms. Well before this, American makers had begun to make news in the industry. The history of the piano in the United States is a story in itself.

Watercolor by Sir Charles D'Oyley (1781–1849) (collection of Mr and Mrs Paul Mellon, Upperville, Virginia, USA). The drawing-room of Sir Charles D'Oyley's bungalow at Bankipur, Patna. Sir Charles was the opium agent and later Commercial Resident at Patna. The piano is a Broadwood.

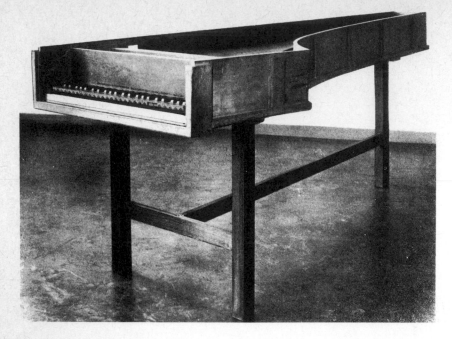

PLATE 51 (*above left*)

Piano by Bartolommeo Cristofori, Florence, Italy, 1726; compass C to c³ (Musikinstrumenten Museum, Karl Marx Universität, Leipzig, Germany). This piano represents the climax of Cristofori's work. It is double-strung, has a synchronized damper system and an *una corda* device, ie a lever underneath the keyboard by means of which one may shift the action so that the hammer strikes only one of a pair of strings for a dynamic contrast. (*Contd*)

PLATE 52 (*left*)

Action of Cristofori's piano of 1726 (Karl Marx Universität, Leipzig). The hammer head is a small block of wood curved on top to hold a hollow cylinder made of layers of thick paper topped with a leather pad for lightness and elasticity.

PLATE 51 (*contd*)

Like harpsichords of the time it is lightly framed and provided with a heavier ornamented case from which it was removed to be played as it is shown here. Its dimensions are virtually the same as those of a harpsichord by the same maker. An examination reveals that Cristofori was indeed a genius, an imaginative craftsman far in advance of his time.

Two other pianos by him survive: one in the Metropolitan Museum of Art, New York, the other in the Museo Degli Strumenti Musicali, Rome.

PLATE 53 (*above centre*)

Grand piano by Gottfried Silbermann, Freiberg, Germany, c. 1745; compass FF to d^3 (Staatliche Schlösser und Garten Potsdam-Sanssouci, Germany). This is one of three Silbermann pianos belonging to Frederick the Great that survived into this century. Two remain in his Sanssouci palace where this one was photographed. The third disappeared but is thought still to be in existence. Silbermann adopted Cristofori's ideas without significant alteration.

PLATE 54 (*left*)

Square piano by Gottlob Emanuel Rüfner, Nürnberg, Germany, c. 1780; compass FF to g^3, two hand stops: one raises dampers, the other is a buff stop moving leather tabs between the hammers and strings (Smithsonian Institution, 332,175, Hugo Worch Collection). The crudely made and painted case of this piano, the keyboard surround covered with stamped paper, is indistinguishable in outward appearance from that of one of the simple clavichords of the time; but instead of a clavichord mechanism it houses a primitive piano action—the *Prellemechanik* or bouncing action.

The hammers are upright wedge-shaped pieces of uncovered wood suggestive of the upright clavichord tangents, but the crucial difference is, of course, that the hammer pivoted to a *kapsel* fixed to the key is propelled up to strike the strings and then permitted to rebound instead of pressing against the strings as long as the key is held down as do the clavichord's tangents. There is no escapement or check.

The maker's name is signed by hand on the label attached to the case behind the keys and he further identifies himself as 'organ and instrument maker of Nürnberg'.

The earliest known surviving square piano with the *Prellemechanik* was made in 1742 by Johann Söcher in Upper Bavaria. It is now in the Germanisches Nationalmuseum, Nürnberg. The sophistication of its craftsmanship suggests that it must have had predecessors. Rüfner was doubtless one of many makers of his time trying his hand at the new instrument. It would be interesting to know if the builders of the earliest of these primitive pianos were, like Cristofori, unconscious of having made a new instrument and, like him, thought of their innovation as an improvement of a familiar one.

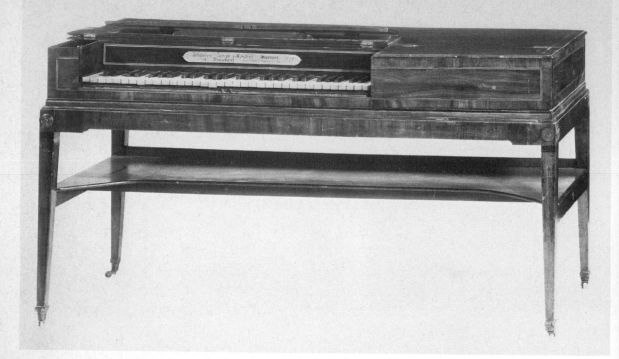

PLATE 55

Square piano by Johannes Zumpe and Gabriel Buntebart, London, 1770; compass FF to f³ (no FF♯) three hand stops: one presses a felt strip against strings in front of hitch-pins for muted effect, a second raises bass dampers and a third raises treble dampers (Smithsonian Institution, 60,1390, formerly Cooper Union Collection, New York). The piano shown here was made during Zumpe's partnership with Gabriel Buntebart (1769–78) and is typical of his instruments. Throughout his career he disdained the more impressive grand model.

The earliest surviving English piano is the one he made in 1766 that has seventeen notes to the octave for most of its compass producing the shade of difference (nearly a quarter-tone) between the sharps and their nearest flats (ie D♯, E♭, F♯, G♭, etc). It recalls the experiments with enharmonic keyboards made in Italy in the seventeenth century and the virginal by Boni shown in plate 36.[34]

Equal temperament had not yet supplanted mean-tone tuning in England, and Zumpe was influenced to make his experimental keyboard by the writings of Dr Robert Smith of Cambridge who advocated twenty four notes to the octave for purer tuning in all keys.

Earlier Johann Sebastian Bach had demonstrated the advantages of a tuning system workable in all keys in his forty-eight Preludes and Fugues for Well-Tempered Clavier and ultimately the general acceptance of equal temperament obviated any need for enharmonic keyboards, and mean-tone tuning was largely forgotten.[35]

PLATE 56

The Cowper and Gore Families, painting by John Zoffany (1734–1810) (property of the Honourable Lady Salmond, Henfield, Sussex, England). This painting of George, 3rd Earl Cowper with his wife, the former Anne Gore, her father and other members of the family, was painted between 1772 and 1776 at the Earl's Florentine villa. Mr Gore is playing the cello held between the knees in the manner of a viola da gamba. It is most likely a piano by Zumpe that is used.[25]

PLATE 57

Grand piano by Johann Andreas Stein, Augsburg; compass FF to f^3, double strung, German action, two knee-levers for raising the dampers (Germanisches Nationalmuseum, Nürnberg, Neupert Collection). The maker is the one whose instruments were much admired by Mozart. This grand piano dates from the 1770s.

PLATE 58

Model of English grand action (Division of Musical Instruments, Smithsonian Institution).

The key A–A is a lever one end of which is struck by the finger. It is held in place by a pin (B) on a fulcrum (K). The hammer (C) is set on the rear end of a shank the front end of which is attached to a small block of wood (O) pivoted to a rail (D) that is part of the frame of the action.

Motion is transmitted to the hammer through the escapement (F), an upright attached to the key. The block of wood at the front of the hammer shank has a notch cut in it that rests on the top of this upright.

When the key is struck the escapement slides back under pressure from the regulating screw (G); when it finally slips out of the notch the hammer that had been travelling up makes its final toss to strike the strings (I). The control of the hammer's upward course until the last instant that is accomplished by the escapement mechanism gives the performer better control over the dynamics than would be possible if the hammer travelled freely from its rest. Once the hammer has struck it drops back against the back-check (E) and remains there as long as the key is held down.

Upon release of the key the back-check moves back allowing the hammer to drop down to its rest (N) and the escapement slips back under the notch in the block of wood as the rear end of the key descends.

The damper system consists of a jack (M) dropped through a mortise in the damper rail, its top capped with a pad of leather and felt (H). The jack is pushed up by the rear end of the key to lift the pad from the strings just before the hammer strikes them. It falls back of its own weight when the key is released.

A Keys
B Pins
C Hammers—the upper one arrested just before the final toss; the other at rest
D Hammer rail (also called hammer beam)
E Back-check
F Escapement (also called hopper or jack)
G Set-off screw to regulate escapement
H Damper
I Strings
J Wrest pins
K Fulcrum
L Hammer shanks
M Damper jack
N Hammer rest
O Notched block of wood (also called butt)

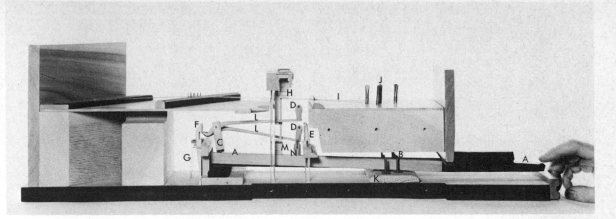

A Keys
B Pins
C Kapsel (hammer support or housing)
D Hammers—the upper one arrested just before the final toss; the other at rest
E Back-check
F Escapement
G Spring
H Damper-jack
I Strings
J Wrest pins
K Fulcrum
L Hammer shanks
M Upright that raises damper jack
N Hammer rest

PLATE 59

Model of German or Viennese action (Division of Musical Instruments, Smithsonian Institution).

The key (A–A) is a lever one end of which is struck by the finger. It is held in place by a pin (B) on a fulcrum (K). The hammer (D) is on the front end of a shank (L) that is pinned at the other end to a Kapsel (C) fixed to the rear of the key. The shank terminates in a beak-shaped projection. The 'beak' rests in a notch in the escapement (F) which is pressed forward at all times by a light spring (G). When the key is struck the Kapsel rises carrying the hammer up and as the beak slips out of the notch in the escapement the hammer is freed to make its final toss to strike the strings (I). The control of the hammer's upward course until the last instant that is accomplished by the escapement mechanism gives the performer better control over the dynamics than would be possible if the hammer travelled freely from its resting place (N) to the strings.

Once the hammer has struck it falls back against the back-check (E) which is covered with material that provides a bit of friction to prevent the hammer from bouncing back to bob undesirably against the strings muffling the tone. It rests there and the beak rests against the escapement above the notch as long as the key is held down. Upon release of the key the hammer drops to its rest (N) as the escapement is pushed back into place by the spring (G).

The damper action consists of two parts: a short base of wood (M) cushioned with felt sits on the key and raises as the key is struck pushing up a damper jack (H) to which is attached a thick pad of felt. The felt lifts from the strings the instant the hammer strikes. When the key is released the jack falls down of its own weight, the felt pad coming to rest again on the strings.

PLATE 60

Mozart and his family. Engraving after a painting by Johann Nepomuk de la Croce, 1781 in Mozart's residence, Salzburg (Internationale Stiftung Mozarteum, Salzburg, Austria). Mozart is seen here at the age of twenty-five playing piano duets with his sister, their father an onlooker and their mother's portrait on the wall. The five-octave compass of the keyboard of the time was scarcely wide enough to accommodate two adults. Mozart had composed his first piece for four hands at one keyboard in 1765 at the age of nine when he and his little sister could quite comfortably fit together at a five-octave harpsichord. One wonders how they managed, comfortably, to play the four-hand compositions he wrote in the 1780s.

Charles Burney, the English music-historian (1726–1814) mentioned this eighteenth-century problem in Rees' *Cyclopaedia* for which he contributed articles on music. 'The ladies at that time wearing hoops which kept them too great a distance from one another had a harpsichord by Merlin[36] expressly for duets with six octaves.' Burney's own duets 'for two Performers upon one Piano Forte or Harpsichord' appear to be the first work for keyboard duet to appear in print and he had one of Merlin's six-octave pianos on which to perform them.[37]

The earliest known composition for two performers at one keyboard is Nicholas Carleton's 'A Verse for Two to Play on one Virginall or Organe' preserved in manuscript in the British Museum and thought to date from the mid-sixteenth century. It has been published in a modern edition.

PLATE 61 *(above left)*

Pedal grand piano. Austrian, late eighteenth century, probably by Johann Schmidt; compass FF to a³, pedalboard, EE/CC to A (bass short octave) (Germanisches Nationalmuseum, Rück Collection, Nürnberg, Germany). Pianos were sometimes equipped with pedalboards as were, earlier, some clavichords, harpsichords and virginals. Pedal pianos, harpsichords and clavichords were intended primarily for organ practice, but Robert Schumann wrote a few compositions especially for pedal piano including six lovely pieces in canon (1845) now heard in transcription for two pianos.

Johann Schmidt was recommended by Mozart's father to the Salzburg court as an organ-builder, and Mozart, therefore, was probably familiar with his instruments.

PLATE 62 *(above right)*

Grand piano by Pascal Taskin, Paris, 1788; compass FF to f³, two knee-levers for raising dampers (Musée Instrumental du Conservatoire National Supérieur de Musique, Paris). Among harpsichord-makers keeping up with the times by making pianos along with harpsichords was Pascal Taskin. This is the earliest of the three grands known to have been made by him. Another dated 1789 is in the Musikinstrumenten-Museum, Staatliches Institut für Musikforschung, Berlin, and the third is in the Petit Trianon, Versailles. The beautiful instrument shown here is indistinguishable, by its outward appearance, from a harpsichord. Its case and the soundboard ornamented with painted flowers are in typical French harpsichord style.

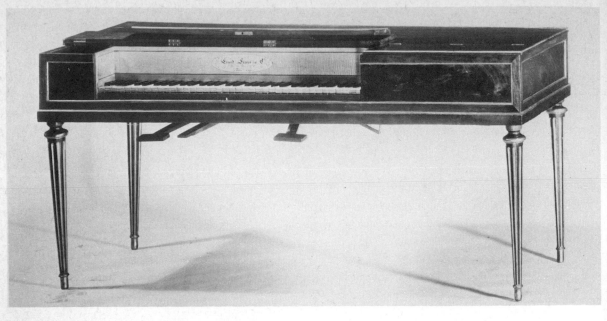

PLATE 64

Mantle clock. Bronze work by Antoine André Ravrio, Paris, 1805-10 (Cooper-Hewitt Museum of Decorative Arts and Design, Smithsonian Institution, New York). The choice of a piano as a decorative motive in this handsome empire-style clock-case suggests the important place the piano had assumed in French society by the early nineteenth century.

PLATE 63 (*facing page, above*)

Square piano by Erard Frères et Cie, Paris, 1799; compass FF to c^4, three knee-levers, one knee-lever raises a flap of the lid for a swell effect, a second raises dampers and the third is a buff stop raising a thin strip of soft leather against the strings (Smithsonian Institution, 315,677, Hugo Worch Collection). The Erard piano illustrated here is equipped with the curious device known as 'nag's head swell' earlier applied to some harpsichords by Jacob Kirckman (see p 50). Impractical when used as intended, it was operated in a novel if unmaidenly way by a certain young lady who, it is reported,[38] owned a pianoforte with two pedals, one for sustaining the sound and the other for opening the short side of the lid for the purpose of obtaining a 'swell' effect. When she played battle pieces she illustrated exploding cannon by suddenly releasing her foot from the swell pedal and permitting the lid to fall with a realistic bang.

PLATE 65

Family of Lucien de Bonaparte, 1815. Drawing by Jean Auguste Dominique Ingres, France, 1786–1867 (Fogg Art Museum, Harvard University, Cambridge, Mass). Here two ladies of the family play lyre guitar and a piano —French instruments evidently taken to Rome by the family upon Lucien's retirement to that city. The drawing was done in Rome.

PLATE 66 (*above left*)

Pyramidal piano by Christian Ernst Friederici, Germany, 1745 (Les Amis du Musée Instrumental du Conservatoire de Musique, Bruxelles). Early experiments in developing a vertical piano were made by Friederici who tried two versions of a pyramidal instrument. In one attributed to him he grouped the long bass strings in the middle and arranged the treble strings on each side, necessitating an action with a kind of tracker system, a mechanism familiar to Friederici from his organ-building. In the later model, shown here and in the following plate, he arranged the strings diagonally over the soundboard. The result was a handsome, but fanciful, instrument.

PLATE 67 (*above right*)

Interior view of the pyramidal piano of the preceding plate.

PLATE 68

Upright grand piano by John Broadwood and Sons, London, c. 1815; compass CC to c⁴, two pedals: *una corda*, and split pedal to raise treble and bass dampers separately if desired (Smithsonian Institution, 303,529, Hugo Worch Collection).

Looking back perhaps to the clavicytherium (plate 26), William Stodart of London brought out in 1795 his 'upright grand': a simple idea in which a small grand is up-ended, installed in a rectangular case and set on a stand. This was more successful than Friederici's earlier idea for a vertical piano (plates 66, 67) and carrying practicality still further, Stodart thoughtfully utilized the space left by the bent side by adding shelves for storing books or music. (*Contd*)

PLATE 69

Interior view of the Broadwood piano shown in the
preceding plate.

The Broadwood piano shown here uses Stodart's plan. The action strikes
from back to front through an opening in the soundboard, a plan equivalent
to the up-striking action usual for a horizontal instrument. Down-striking
action was tried from time to time in horizontal instruments, but was
abandoned due to the difficulty of achieving a prompt rebound. Before the
end of the nineteenth century, however, a front-to-back action became
standard in principle for uprights.

The split damper pedal for controlling treble and bass dampers separately
suggests interesting possibilities for use when one hand is called upon to
play *staccato* and the other *legato*. Beethoven's piano of 1817 (plate 71) and
the early grand of 1811 in plate 72 have such an arrangement. (*Contd*)

It was ultimately discarded.

As with the upright harpsichord or clavicytherium, the action of the vertical piano must have a spring mechanism to aid the hammers and dampers to fall back into place, since this is not accomplished by the force of gravity as is the case in the horizontal instruments.

This piano stands nearly 9ft tall and is threateningly top heavy.

PLATE 70

Grand piano by Sébastien Erard, Paris, 1801; compass FF to c⁴, four pedals, one *una corda* knee-lever (Finchcocks Collection, Richard Burnett, Goudhurst, Kent). The four pedals are: bassoon on lower strings; damper; moderator (which moves forward felt tabs through which the hammers then strike; each tab is graduated in thickness and an extremely subtle gradation of dynamics can be achieved by slowly depressing and releasing the pedal); *due corda*. (The bassoon pedal is explained on p95.)

Except for the knee-lever this is like the piano the Erard firm presented to Beethoven in 1803. He was never fond of it and it can be conjectured that one reason was the complicated pedal system. Although extraordinary coloristic effects can be achieved with the four pedals, they are tricky to use.

PLATE 71

Grand piano by John Broadwood and Sons, London, 1817; compass CC to c^4, two pedals: *una corda* and split pedal for controlling treble and bass dampers separately (National Museum, Budapest, Hungary). This piano was the one given to Beethoven by the Broadwoods.

PLATE 72 (*above left*)

Piano by Broadwood and Sons, London, 1811; and *The Sisters*. Painting by Sir William Beechey, England, c. 1830 (Huntington Galleries, George L. Bagby Collection, Huntington, West Virginia). The piano in the foreground of this photograph is a near twin in all important respects to the one illustrated in the preceding plate. It was obviously a proud possession.

PLATE 73 (*above right*)

Giraffe piano by Martin Seuffert, Vienna, c. 1812; compass FF to f⁴, two pedals: *una corda* and damper (Smithsonian Institution, 315,657, Hugo Worch Collection). In the piano presented here the case adheres to the shape of the up-ended grand, unlike the Broadwood in plates 68 and 69. A good number of these so-called giraffe pianos were made, many with quite handsomely decorated cases, their elegance belying the incongruous appellation that was applied to them.

PLATE 74

Upright piano by Wilkinson and Wornum, London, c. 1812; compass FF to c⁴, two pedals: one slides pads of felt against strings for a muted effect, a second raises dampers (Smithsonian Institution, 315,673, Hugo Worch Collection). Many designs for small pianos were tried. A model patented by the English maker, William Collard, in 1798, was simply a square piano turned up on its side and placed on a stand. William Southwell's 'piano sloping backward' was a similar arrangement, but with the piano tipped back from the performer; the designer claimed that his model was more comfortable for the performer and obligingly equipped it with a device for turning pages by means of a pedal.

The piano shown here is an early example of the small pianos introduced by Robert Wornum. The back is covered with the same wood and finished in the same way as the front and sides so that the instrument may be seen from any angle and need not be placed against the wall as with the usual uprights. Since this piano is only 41in tall the performer's head could be seen above, a particular advantage to the self-accompanied singer.

In 1813 Wornum brought out a small upright with vertical stringing reaching to the floor and utilizing all the available space, a type which he called a 'Cottage' piano. In 1838 he listed a variety of other models: the 'Piccolo' which stood 3ft 8in, the 'Cabinet' (ie tall upright), the 'Pocket Grand Horizontal', only 5ft 4in long, and the 'Imperial Grand Horizontal'.[39] The small pianos were copied by European makers, including Pleyel in France who called them 'Pianinos'.

PLATE 75

Table piano made by Jean-Henri Pape, Paris, mid-nineteenth century; compass FF to f⁴, two pedals; formerly the property of the Duke of Wellington (Gallini Collection, Civico Museo Degli Strumenti Musicali, Castello Sforzesco, Milano, Italy). For a time there was a vogue for dual-purpose pianos—miniature boudoir- or sewing-tables, or writing-desks, the tops of which opened to reveal the piano keys of their secret musical lives.

Jean-Henri Pape can be forgiven the ungainly piece of furniture housing this piano if one recalls that he patented many ideas aimed at improving piano action, and that he made, in 1826, a very significant contribution by his development of a satisfactory felt for covering the hammers—the first time felt replaced deer skin for this purpose. In 1839 he designed a hammer-cover of tapered layers of treated felt—the type still in use. German makers were the last to give up the deer skin covering and resisted the use of felt until the early 1850s. The hammers of a modern grand piano developed from Pape's ideas are shown in plate 98.

PLATE 76

Liszt at the Piano. Painting by Joseph Danhauser, Vienna, 1840 (National Galerie der Stiftung Preussischer Kulturbesitz, Berlin). This purports to be a painting of Liszt with Alexandre Dumas and Georges Sand, seated, Victor Hugo, Paganini and Rossini, standing, and the Countess d'Agoult swooning in ecstasy, her head against the piano. A bust of Beethoven, also by Danhauser, dominates the scene. A photograph of Lord Byron hangs on the wall.

The instrument shows the mark of Conrad Graf, well-known Viennese maker. This realistic touch notwithstanding, the presence of Victor Hugo arouses a suspicion that the painting does not record an actual event. Hugo did not like music and when some of his poems were set to music asked disdainfully, 'Why, aren't they musical enough?'[40]

PLATE 77

Liszt et Son Sabre. From *La Vie Parisienne*, 3 April 1886 (Library of Congress, Washington, DC). Liszt fully exploited the tonal resources of the piano both in his compositions and performances. His extravagant flamboyant style and his assaults upon the keyboard are caricatured here with the translated caption:

> LISZT AND HIS SWORD—that he has renounced today, after having recognised that he was doing more harm to the piano with his hands alone. Strange specimen of the race of creatures with tentacles. Eight hands with four octaves each, thirty-two octaves!!![41]

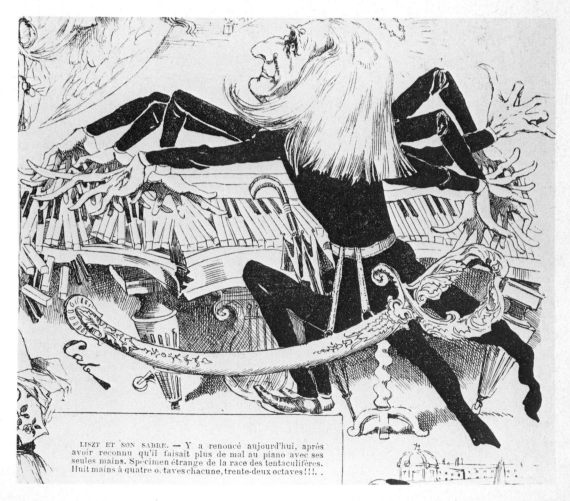

LISZT ET SON SABRE. — Y a renoncé aujourd'hui, après avoir reconnu qu'il faisait plus de mal au piano avec ses seules mains. Spécimen étrange de la race des tentaculifères. Huit mains à quatre octaves chacune, trente-deux octaves!!!.

PLATE 78

Grand piano by Ignace Pleyel et Cie, France; compass CC to g⁴ (Pleyel Collection, Paris). This piano once belonged to Frédéric Chopin and it is said that he used it when composing many of his great piano works, including some of the Préludes, the G minor Nocturne, Op 37, No 1, the funeral march of the B minor Sonata, Op 34 and the F minor Fantasie Op 49, and that his last concert in February 1848 was played on this instrument.

PLATE 79

Joseph Joachim and Clara Schumann, 1854. Drawing by Adolph von Menzel, Germany, 1815–1905 (Staatsbibliothek, Berlin). Clara Schumann's favorite piano is said to have been one by Grotrian-Steinweg—the firm founded by Theodore Steinweg who remained in Germany when his father and brothers came to the United States to found the Steinway firm under their Americanized name. Here she is accompanying the famous violinist Joseph Joachim who performed often with Clara Schumann's life-long friend, Johannes Brahms, at the piano.

PLATE 80

Upright piano by Pleyel, Paris, 1857–8; compass AAA to a⁴, two pedals: *una corda*, damper (Smithsonian Institution, 291,775, Hugo Worch Collection). Lavishly decorated in a manner derived from the masterpieces of André Charles Boulle, celebrated cabinet-maker of Louis XIV's time, this small upright piano is covered with red imitation tortoise-shell and brass inlay. It has an ornate brass handle on each side and delicate candelabras with pale-pink glass shades. A few of the small pianos popular at this date were ornamented in this extravagant style.

PLATE 81

Young Girls at the Piano. Painting by Auguste Renoir, France, 1892 (The Lehman Collection, New York). The young French girls in this painting are pleasurably engaged in making music at a small piano of the type made popular by Pleyel. It recalls the one in the preceding plate.

87

6

IN AMERICA

THE ADVENT OF THE PIANO IN AMERICA

In the first New England settlements in the seventeenth century the hardships of life and the stern attitude of the Puritans towards worldly pleasures inhibited musical pursuits. Nevertheless the harsh Puritan attitude toward music has often been exaggerated. They brought with them their psalm tunes and their enthusiasm for psalm singing, and they permitted themselves the enjoyment of instrumental music in the privacy of their homes, although they frowned on its use in church. Disapproved by many, dancing and fiddling were, however, indulged in by some. The few musical instruments in use had been brought from home or were sent on a later ship.

That these conditions did not prevail for long is indicated by an advertisement in a Boston newspaper of 1716[42] announcing the arrival of various musical instruments and instruction books, and offering repair of musical instruments including tuning and stringing of virginalls [sic] and spinnets [sic].

Music had assumed an important place in the life of a cultured American family by the middle of the eighteenth century. The first public concert took place in Boston in 1731 and other concerts, as well as theatrical performances, soon followed. Charleston, South Carolina, followed Boston's lead with a public concert and in 1736 New York boasted a concert arranged by a German, Charles Theodore Pachelbel, who had served as church organist in Newport, Rhode Island; Pachelbel himself was at the harpsichord.

A group of Moravians fleeing from religious persecution in Bohemia brought to America their customary performances of chamber music, symphonies and oratorios, a tradition that has been preserved uninterrupted to the present time in Bethlehem, Pennsylvania and Winston-Salem, North Carolina.

A clavichord in the Smithsonian Institution collection was brought to this country in 1741 by one of their members, and as early as 1743 the Moravian brethren had a small orchestra that included violins, viols, flutes, and French horns. These were played for the first time in the house of God at Bethlehem for the Christmas feast of that year. In 1744 a spinet from England was added. In 1765 a Mohican Indian living in a community set up for Christian Indians, built a spinet with the help of one of the missionaries. It was used in chapel services and to accompany the singing of Delaware Indian hymns. In 1792 a charge of '£7–10sh for repairing and tuning seven pianos and clavichords in the Boarding School' at Bethlehem is recorded.[43]

The Moravians' Collegium Musicum founded in 1744 was the first such organization in this country, and string quartets composed by the Moravian, Johann Peter, in 1789 appear to be the oldest chamber music composed on American soil.

Musical activities and musical instruments were an important part of gracious living in the colonial South and ample historical records suggest that the South was richer in music than New England. Harpsichords and spinets could be found in a fair number of houses and pianos were not unknown. Colonel Robert Carter, a Virginia gentleman, accomplished musician, and owner of one of the most beautiful plantations in all the South, added a piano to his extensive collection of musical instruments in 1771. In the same year Thomas Jefferson countermanded his order for a clavichord from England with one for a piano. Francis Hopkinson, signer of the Declaration of Independence, ordered a Shudi and Broadwood harpsichord in 1783 with a request that it be quilled in an 'improved manner' he had devised. George Washington acquired a harpsichord from the firm of Longman and Broderip of London in 1793 that is still preserved in his house at Mount Vernon. The last two dates indicate that at least some Americans were slower than Europeans to accept pianos in place of harpsichords.

A few spinets were made on American soil by foreigners, including the German, Johann Gottlieb Klemm, whose spinet, made in Philadelphia in 1739, is in the collection of the Metropolitan Museum. John Harris, a well-known Londoner who emigrated here in 1768, made at least one spinet in this country; but one of 1789 in the Essex Institute Museum, Salem, Massachusetts, is by native-born Samuel Blythe.

A concert in which a piano, almost certainly an English import, was used, was given in New York as early as 1773.

Through the last quarter of the century, a considerable number of pianos, sometimes listed as 'hammer harpsichords', were arriving in the eastern ports from London along with other cargo. In 1789 John Jacob Astor began to export furs and brought back some pianos on the return journeys, both to defray expenses and to act as agent for his brother who was dealing in pianos in London. A newspaper account of 1791[44] stated that at least twenty-seven Boston families owned pianos, all of them London made.

The first piano produced on the North American continent was probably made by John Behrent, a German immigrant living in Philadelphia. In 1775 he announced 'an extraordinary instrument, by the name of the piano-forte, in mahogany in the manner of the harpsichord'.[45] By 1785 pianos were commonly made in New York.

Then about 1798 Benjamin Crehore founded the 'Boston school' of piano-makers in nearby Milton, Massachusetts. He had as apprentices Alpheus Babcock and John Osborn. Osborn in turn took James Stewart, a Scot, and Jonas Chickering of New Hampshire, into his own shop. All made important contributions to piano-making and their names will reappear later in this chapter.

Meanwhile, a number of makers from England and the Continent were coming to try their luck on American soil and from 1800 on American piano industry rapidly gained momentum. Native enterprise and ingenuity combined with the influence of the experienced foreigners contributed to its success.

As to the earliest American contribution to literature for the keyboard, Hopkinson's eight songs to be accompanied by harpsichord or piano are something of a milestone. They were engraved in Philadelphia in 1788, the first music involving harpsichord and piano to be published in this country. Hopkinson claimed to have been the first native of the United States to produce a musical composition; two of his earlier works date from 1754 and 1759.

Pretty little square pianos were arriving in considerable numbers from England in the eighteenth century (plate 83) and by 1790 Charles Albrecht (presumably of German origin) was making fine little squares in Philadelphia (plate 84)—copies, with minor improvements, of the English pianos coming from London and scarcely distinguishable from them. It was not long before a number of makers were established. The collection of keyboard instruments in the Smithsonian Institution contains 113 square pianos; and of those made before 1835, 56 are American, 30 are English, 9 German, 2 French, 2 Dutch and 2 Austrian. If it can be assumed that most of them were in use in the United States before they came to the collection, the proportion suggests that well before the middle of the nineteenth century American-made pianos were successfully competing with the imported ones. Pianos soon became the rage, piano-makers proliferated astonishingly and every American family with pretensions to culture, an interest in music, and enough money to buy one was determined to have a piano in the parlor (plate 92).

JOHN HAWKINS AND THE UPRIGHT PIANO

Towards the end of the eighteenth century John Isaac Hawkins, a young English engineer with an inventive turn of mind,[46] emigrated to Philadelphia and began to concern himself with innovations in piano construction, as his father had done in England. He patented several piano stops for novel effects, but most important was his design for an upright piano, the credit for the development of which he shares with Mathias Müller of Vienna, who brought out a similar instrument in precisely the same year, 1800. The vertical instrument of William Stodart and others (see plate 68) had been scarcely more than a conventional piano turned upright and placed on a stand. The Hawkins and Muller pianos utilized the space extending to the floor by running the strings vertically from top to bottom inside a surprisingly small rectangular case (as seen in plate 87). This stringing plan with the addition of over-stringing as well and also a front-to-back striking action applied to larger instruments created the type of upright piano without which, by the end of the nineteenth century, no American middle-class home was complete.

The Hawkins piano (plate 86) is noteworthy for a metal frame in which the soundboard is suspended and for a metal-covered wrestpin block—probably the first such use of metal. Although there is no evidence that Hawkins influenced other makers—his piano was in fact a failure as a musical instrument—his work reflects contemporary interest in experiments to solve the problems created by the increasing demands made on the piano.[47]

ALPHEUS BABCOCK

In 1825 Alpheus Babcock, a Boston maker who worked for a time in Philadelphia, produced a complete metal frame cast in one with the hitchpin block (plates 88, 89). Although Hawkins had used already iron bracing and Broadwood had made a piano in 1821 with two iron bars in the treble and one in 1825 with an iron frame under the soundboard, in general, resistance to iron framing had amounted almost to phobia. Its universal adoption at a later date, however, proved to be the answer to the problems that had been plaguing makers and performers.

Babcock deserves further credit for promoting the use of cross-stringing or over-stringing. Although the principle did not originate from him, his plan had far-reaching influence. It involved running the long bass strings diagonally above the others, so making more effective use of the available space. It can be seen in a later piano by Steinway (plate 94).

JONAS CHICKERING

The first great name in American piano-making is Jonas Chickering. In 1817 Chickering, 19-year-old cabinet-maker's apprentice and son of a blacksmith and farmer in New Ipswich, New Hampshire, was summoned to make emergency repairs to a piano that had belonged to Princess Amelia, youngest daughter of George III. The young man was musically inclined, could play fife and clarinet and had taught himself to read music, but he had had no experience in repairing musical instruments. Spurred by the challenge, however, he accomplished the task and, emboldened by his success, he set off not long after for Boston. After working for a year with a Boston cabinet-maker, he persuaded John Osborn, a leading piano-maker of the time, to hire him. Joinery, or cabinet-making, is solid training for the more esoteric craft of musical-instrument making—it has been the stepping-stone to such a career for many another—and the Osborn-Chickering association was fortuitous for both men.

In 1823, James Stewart, a young Scot who had been making pianos in Baltimore and Philadelphia, came to work in Osborn's shop but soon quarrelled with him and proposed that Chickering should join him in setting up their own shop. They worked together for three successful years before Stewart left for London to join the established firm of Collard & Collard, taking with him some of the Stewart-Chickering pianos, no doubt the first American pianos seen there. Stewart introduced a method of stringing used by the Boston makers and thereafter exchange of ideas between American and English makers was lively.

After a few years on his own Chickering again acquired a partner in John Mackay, a sea-captain and sharp businessman. Mackay set about making Chickering pianos known in the major cities of the United States and on voyages to South America took pianos with him, bringing back rosewood and mahogany for the shop. Mackay was lost at sea in 1841 but by this time the firm was on solid footing.

The problems of maintaining a wood-framed piano described earlier were occupying the attention of every maker. Babcock's metal frame for the square piano may have given Chickering the idea for an improved cast-iron frame that he patented in 1840 for the square piano and, in 1843, developed further for the grand model. These were the real 'break-through'. At the first International Exhibition held in the Crystal Palace in London in 1851, they created a sensation.

While it remained for the Steinways with their widely acclaimed piano exhibited at the fair of the American Institute in 1855 to win incontestably the 'battle of the iron frame' and demonstrate that a piano with a cast-iron frame could indeed produce the desired tonal quality and volume, it was none other than William Steinway who hailed Chickering as 'the father of American pianoforte making'. Few would take issue with a more sweeping apellation: 'the father of the modern pianoforte'. A contemporary described him as 'upright, square and grand like his own pianos'. The piano shown in plate 91 incorporates the iron frame although it was made three years before Chickering took out his patent for it.

Chickering died prematurely in 1853, but not before he had started a gigantic new factory (the old one having been levelled by fire) and had taken his three sons as partners. The new plant, superbly planned and equipped, was said at the time to be the largest building on the continent apart from the United States Capitol. The sons were well educated, trained by their father in his craft and dedicated to carrying on the fine tradition he had established. The Chickering firm was the undisputed leader in the field at this date, producing more than a thousand pianos a year and it had become the first major exporter of pianos.

Honors and recognition came to the Chickerings from all over the western world through the next decades. In 1867 the Emperor Napoleon III awarded to C. Frank Chickering the Imperial Cross of the Legion of Honor for his 'distinguished service to the art of music' after Chickering pianos had won the highest awards at the great Paris Exposition. The maker then proceeded to Rome to present a piano to Franz Liszt who pronounced it 'imperial', saying, 'I never thought a piano could possess such qualities.' The Norwegian composer, Edvard Grieg, recalled playing for Liszt on 'the glorious Chickering'. Indeed, every great musician of the second half of the nineteenth century knew and admired Chickering pianos.

The last of Jonas Chickering's sons died in 1896, leaving no member of the family to carry on the business and in 1908 the firm was absorbed by the Aeolian-American Corporation.

STEINWAY AND SONS

The year 1853 is significant in American piano history. In this year the Chickering firm was at its zenith and the Steinways began making pianos in a modest establishment in New York.

Steinway family legend has it that the founder of their firm, Heinrich Engelhard Steinweg, while serving as apprentice to an organ-builder and organist in the village church of Seesen, Germany, made a piano as a spare-time project in his kitchen in 1836. He presented it to his wife and it is still in the possession of their descendants.

Steinweg prospered as a repairer and tuner of organs and made such progress in piano-making that he was able to exhibit one grand and two squares at the Brunswick Fair in 1839.

The five sons of Heinrich Steinweg were working with him when in 1849 the middle one, forced to flee for political reasons, came to America. He was intrigued with the possibilities in the New World and soon persuaded his father and three of the brothers to join him. They all worked at first in different piano factories in New York and studied the English language, the father changing his name to Henry Engelhard Steinway. Finally they opened their own shop and from the beginning the venture was happy and successful. Only a year after the Steinway & Sons firm was established it received a prize for a square piano at the Metropolitan Fair held in Washington. The next year, 1855, its over-strung square piano with a full iron frame created a sensation at the fair of the American Institute; nothing so fine had ever been heard and resistance to iron framing was once and for all overcome. An example of such a piano is shown in plates 93 and 94.

Every important maker both here and abroad had been experimenting since the early 1800s with the use of metal reinforcing bars. The Broadwoods in 1847 developed a grand piano frame with iron diagonal tension and transverse suspension bars that was deemed so satisfactory that they continued making it for nearly fifty years. There had also been Babcock's iron frame for a square piano and Chickering's for a grand, but it was the

Steinway iron frame of 1855 adapted for grand pianos a few years later that became the model for future pianos.

By 1859 business had expanded so rapidly that the Steinways found it necessary to erect a huge factory in New York planned and supervised by the father with as much care as he lavished on the pianos themselves. The Steinway piano was recognized at the Paris Exposition of 1867 as a distinct type worthy to take its place beside those of fine English and continental makers (plate 95).

PIANO STYLES AND EXPERIMENTS

Square and upright pianos were becoming more and more numerous in American homes. Almost every family with the means and any pretensions to culture managed to acquire one. The grand piano, however, remained something of a novelty in the hinterlands.

When the New-Orleans-born composer and piano virtuoso Louis Moreau Gottschalk was making a barnstorming tour in 1862 accompanied by two specially built Chickering grands, an 'honest farmer' asked him after a performance somewhere in Indiana what that 'big accordion' was. He had seen squares and uprights but the grand shape puzzled him.

At a concert in Zanesville, Ohio, the pianist was disconcerted by a 'charming young girl and her honorable mama' who passed the whole of the concert in watching his feet from their front row seats. It transpired that they did not know the use of the pedals and saw in the movement of the feet a 'kind of queer trembling, and odd and rudimentary steps in dancing which, for two hours and a quarter, afforded them an inexhaustible source of amusement'.

When Gottschalk was once forced to play a concert on a square piano because his two grands had not arrived, he wrote: 'On commencing I cast a look of pity on it. "Poor little thing; thou dost not know what awaits thee." But the valiant little piano did not flinch and sustained the assault without losing a string or a hammer.'[48]

Although successful grands were being made in America by several manufacturers for some time, the demand for this model was limited and even affluent families inexplicably continued to acquire squares rather than emulate European taste for finer and more impressive grands (plate 92). By 1876 about one-sixth of the Steinway output consisted of grands and they made their last square in 1889—perhaps the last made in the United States. By 1900 the grand piano had become the accepted model for serious musicians and the concert stage and by 1904 square pianos had become such an embarassment to the industry that the manufacturers at their congress in Atlantic City acquired a number of them and ceremoniously set fire to them.

Meanwhile, uprights, already the prevalent economy model in Europe, had been replacing squares and the ubiquitous American reed organ that had enjoyed a vogue, especially in rural areas, as accompaniment for family and friendly groups singing hymns and popular ballads.

Toward the end of the eighteenth century some piano-makers came under the spell of the fad for music of the Janissary guard of Turkish sovereigns. This military body had marched for several centuries to big drums, cymbals, triangles, and the Turkish crescent or 'Jingling Johnny', a pole to which were attached bells and crescents of metal to produce a rousing percussive din. The sound became so popular that other European rulers assembled in the eighteenth and nineteenth centuries their own 'Turkish' bands or introduced Turkish elements into their regimental bands. Mozart, Beethoven and others wrote worthy music in the Turkish style; some carried the idea even to the point of writing battle pieces with effects imitating the sound of cannons, clashing sabers, or galloping horses.

During some forty years of the nineteenth century, multiple pedals—as many as six—were attached to a considerable number of pianos of all shapes to imitate the Janissary sound. A typical arrangement of pedals, starting from left to right, is the following: (1) 'bassoon' which brings a slip of parchment into contact with the lowest three octaves causing a kind of buzzing sound; (2) a pedal operating a drum-stick that beats on the underside of the soundboard; (3) triangles and cymbals; (4) celeste soft pedal placing felt strips in front of hammers; (5) shifting *una corda* pedal; (6) damper pedal. The practice of adding bizarre effects was prolonged as piano transcriptions of orchestral works became popular.

The first patents for these gadgets were English, but European as well as American makers (plate 85) succumbed to them. The ultimate must have been a piano with chromatic kettledrums, patented in 1847 by Nunns & Fisher, New York.

The phenomenon described here is a debasement of the piano, mentioned only because it existed; it is best forgotten.

While the modern piano was being developed, a number of unsuccessful experiments were made. Most interesting among them was the Janko keyboard, which had no ultimate influence on the present-day piano, but reflected makers' concern with solving performance problems as well as the structural problems of the piano.

In 1882 Paul von Janko, a Hungarian musician and engineer patented a keyboard with six banks of short keys (plate 96). It was introduced by a Viennese piano-maker a few years later and in turn taken up by some American makers. Each row is tuned in the whole-tone scale: rows 1, 3, and 5 beginning with C; 2, 4 and 6 with C♯. The six rows constitute one keyboard operating on the same set of strings. Among the advantages attributed to it were that it compensated for the unequal lengths of the fingers, all diatonic scales could be played with only two sets of fingerings, and the octave span being smaller the hand could encompass a much greater stretch for widely spaced chords. The invention aroused some interest, claiming a few adherents, and a school was established in New York in 1891 to teach the method of playing it; but along with some other less well-conceived experiments, the Janko keyboard was abandoned after a few years. To the pianist whose ten fingers on occasions are either too many or too few, depending on the technical problem of the moment, multiple keyboards proved to be of no help.

Other experimental pianos worthy of passing notice were those with octave couplers on which a performer could play on one or another of the sets of strings or couple the two actions together much in the manner of the two manual harpsichords of earlier times. Erard Frères experimented in this direction in the early 1800s and in 1921 Emanuel Moor, a Hungarian-born pianist and inventor, brought out the Moor-Duplex piano with two keyboards an octave apart. Steinway, Bechstein, and Bösendorfer incorporated this mechanism into a few pianos and Moor's wife, the English pianist Winifred Christie, gave performances using the Moor keyboard in Europe and America. Interest in it waned with her disappearance from the concert scene.

American manufacturers willing to try anything to attract business in a highly competitive market, experimented with various kinds of novel musical instruments and at least one of them made a few so-called 'harp pianos' (plate 90). Omitting a soundboard, they stood the frame upright exposing its picturesque shape, unenclosed by a case and provided it with a hammer action. It satisfied no demands.

Well before the turn of the century, the American grand piano had achieved its modern form in all essential details. Its action is an awesome feat of engineering containing nearly 12,000 individual parts (plates 97, 98, 99). It was evolved over more than two hundred years through the combined ingenuity, imagination and labor of numerous inventors and craftsmen. The story of its success is inextricably bound up with the Steinway family, its members working in unbroken line since the founding of their firm and in constant communication with great pianists and scientists. Although fine pianos are made by many firms in America and abroad, the indebtedness of the profession to the Steinways is generally recognized. Many pianists prefer their pianos over all others. Their 100,000th piano presented with understandable pride to the White House in 1903 (plate 100) commemorated the fiftieth year of their successful career.

PLATE 82

At the Piano. Painting by James McNeill Whistler (1834–1903) (Taft Museum, Cincinnati, Ohio). In 1859 Whistler, in London on a visit from Paris, painted his half-sister, the wife of the well-known etcher and surgeon, Francis Seymour Haden. The little girl is her daughter. The family preoccupation with music is emphasized by the rapt attention of the figures at the piano and, further, by the inclusion of the cello case and what appears to be a violin case under the piano as part of the composition. Evidently the room was a setting for chamber music.

The large grand piano is unidentified as to maker, but it is probably a Broadwood, as the style of the legs and the carved keyboard brackets are similar to those of some mid-nineteenth-century pianos by this firm.

PLATE 83 (*facing page, above*)

Square piano by Culliford, Rolfe and Barrow, London, c. 1790; compass FF to f³, two hand-stops: one for raising dampers from treble strings, the other from bass strings (Smithsonian Institution, 315,664, Hugo Worch Collection). This is typical of the pianos which were arriving in America in considerable numbers in the late eighteenth century. It is light in weight and can be easily lifted from its stand.

PLATE 84 (*facing page, below*)

Square piano by Charles Albrecht, Philadelphia, c. 1798; compass FF to f³, one hand-stop for raising the dampers (Smithsonian Institution, 288,399, Hugo Worch Collection). This piano contains the English double action, but Albrecht installed the German action in some of his other pianos, one of only a few American makers to do so. The influence of the English makers is reflected in the style of the case as well as in the mechanism.

PLATE 85

Square piano by A. Reuss, Cincinnati, Ohio, 1832–5; compass FF to f⁴, four pedals operating left to right as follows: bassoon stop, raises dampers, buff stop, bass drum and bells (Smithsonian Institution, 315,721, Hugo Worch Collection). The extraordinary pedal equipment of this early nineteenth-century piano is due to the fad that developed at the end of the eighteenth century for music of the Janissary, described on p95.

PLATE 86

Portable grand piano by John Isaac Hawkins, Philadelphia, 1801; compass
FF to f³, two pedals: a Venetian swell and a buff stop (Smithsonian Institution, 313,619, Hugo Worch Collection). The keyboard of this piano folds
up into a little portable cabinet with carrying handles on each side. Along
with some new ideas (described pp90–1) incorporated into the structure
of this piano, Hawkins revived some old ones. One pedal, instead of
raising the dampers—as would be expected—operates a Venetian swell, a
device invented by Burkat Shudi and used in the harpsichord in plate 50.
Equally surprising is the reappearance of boxwood to cover the natural
keys. It had been customarily used for this purpose in Italian harpsichords;
the instruments in plates 27, 36 and 37 have boxwood naturals and ebony
accidentals. Other woods and other materials such as tortoise shell and
mother-of-pearl were sometimes chosen (see plate 47) and the keys of a few
instruments were decorated with inlaid designs. Ebony for naturals and

bone for the tops of accidentals were commonly in use in France in the eighteenth century. Flemish seventeenth-century makers and the English were inclined to a reversal of this contrast and usually covered the naturals with bone or ivory and made the accidentals of ebony. The eighteenth-century Flemish harpsichord in plate 39, the French in plate 44, and the Stein piano in plate 57 all have ebony naturals and bone-capped accidentals. The spinet by Hitchcock in plate 38 has a stripe of ivory set into each ebony accidental, a favorite conceit of this maker. A few late nineteenth-century American heavy square pianos with elaborately carved and painted cases were fitted out with mother-of-pearl covered naturals.

The choice of material for keyboards seems to have been early a question of materials at hand and later one of individual preference, although the unlikely theory has been set forth that ebony naturals were selected for the purpose of showing off to advantage feminine white hands. In any event, around the beginning of the nineteenth century ivory naturals and ebony accidentals became standard; in recent years, however, a fine quality of plastic has been substituted for ivory.

Thomas Jefferson bought one of Hawkins' upright pianos for his Virginia mansion 'Monticello', but soon afterwards wrote to complain that it would not stay in tune even for an hour. Hawkins replied that he was not surprised, that he realized what the trouble was and could correct it if the piano were returned to him. Pecuniary embarrassment necessitated making a charge of $40 which he would repay after he arrived in England. Meanwhile Jefferson had read of Hawkins' new invention, the 'claviola', and thought he might like to trade the piano for one. Hawkins had no claviola available, however, and proposed exchanging the piano for another at a cost of $300 allowing for an original purchase price at $250. The correspondence does not reveal how all this was resolved.

The claviola deserves a word as an experimental keyboard instrument. Its keyboard compass is two octaves and two notes and it contains a perpendicular viol-shaped soundboard across which are stretched wire strings. In front a guide sliding along a brass rod holds a violin bow. On pressing a key the string is raised and brought in contact with the bow. Hawkins made extravagant claims for the beauty of its sounds. It recalls some experiments described earlier that were made with harpsichords in the seventeenth century.

These instruments of Hawkins were not successful musically, but they suggest contemporary interest in experimenting with improvements.

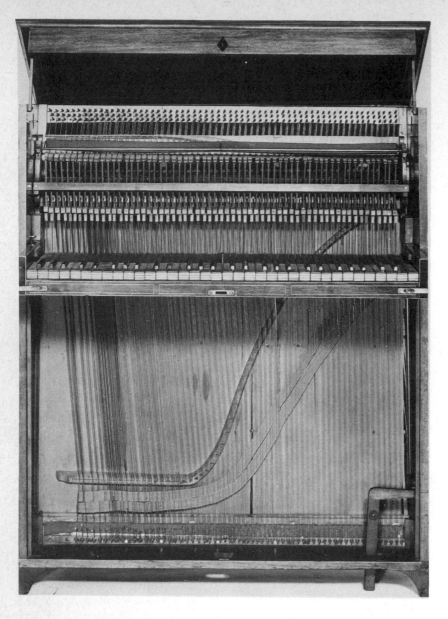

PLATE 87

Interior view of the piano illustrated in the preceding plate.

PLATE 88 (*facing page, above*)

Square piano by Alpheus Babcock made at William Swift's Piano Forte Manufactory, Philadelphia, c. 1835; compass FF to f⁴, two pedals: one slides felt between hammers and strings, the other controls dampers (Smithsonian Institution, 315,690, Hugo Worch Collection). This piano has a complete metal frame cast in one piece—a revolutionary idea at the time. The greater weight of the instrument with iron framing necessitates increasing the size of the legs. Acceptance of the iron frame was

slow, but when it caught on, the graceful little square pianos with spindly legs such as those in plates 83 and 84 could no longer be made. A square piano can often be quite precisely dated simply on the basis of the style of its legs. Babcock has managed to design here an attractive piece of furniture, but some later makers, not so well endowed with taste, produced many square pianos supported by monstrously large and ugly legs.

PLATE 89

Plan view showing the tubular iron frame of the piano by Alpheus Babcock in the preceding plate.

PLATE 90
Harp piano, probably by Kuhn and Ridgeway, Baltimore, 1857; compass CC to c⁵, two pedals: *una corda*, damper (Smithsonian Institution, 299,854, Hugo Worch Collection). This experimental instrument had a very short life.

PLATE 92 (*facing page, below*)

Mr and Mrs Ernest Fiedler and Family. Painting by Franz Heinrich, New York, c. 1846 (collection of Mrs William L. Rich, New York). In an opulent setting such as this, one would expect to find a grand piano, but the square model continued in favor in the United States for most of the nineteenth century long after it had been given up for the upright and grand models in England and on the continent.

PLATE 91

Concert grand piano by Chickering, Boston, 1840; compass CC to c⁵, two pedals: *una corda*, damper (formerly Henry Ford Museum, Dearborn, Michigan). This piano with its handsome rosewood case is the first grand made by Chickering. It contains the successful cast-iron frame that he patented three years later.

PLATE 93

Square piano by Steinway & Sons, New York, 1877–8; compass AAA to c⁵,
two pedals: *una corda*, damper (Smithsonian Institution, 381,444, Hugo
Worch Collection). A piano of the type that made history at the American
Institute in 1855 and created a sensation at the Paris Exposition of 1867.

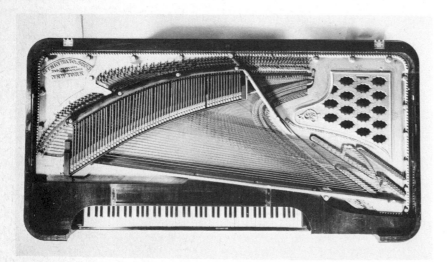

PLATE 94

Plan view showing the full
iron plate and over-stringing of the Steinway piano
in the previous plate.

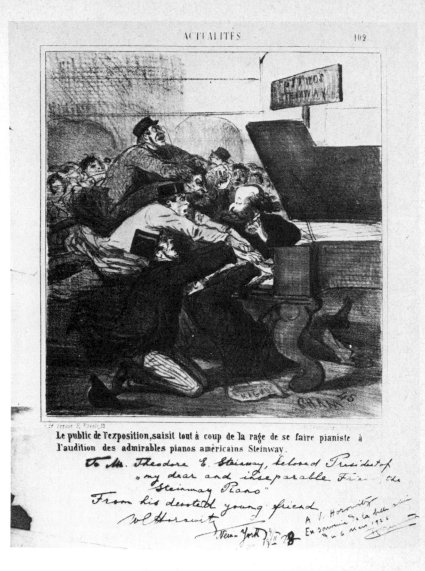

Le public de l'exposition, saisit tout à coup de la rage de se faire pianiste à l'audition des admirables pianos américains Steinway.

To Mr. Theodore E. Steinway, beloved President of "my dear and inseparable Friend, the Steinway Piano". From his devoted young friend, Wl Horowitz. New-York 15/III 28. À V. Horowitz En souvenir de la belle soirée du 6 Mars 1926.

PLATE 95

Lithograph by Amédée de Noé ('Cham'), Paris, c. 1867 (collection Steinway & Sons). The Steinways applied the principles of iron framing and over-stringing to the grand piano in 1859 and favorable articles about their new piano appeared in European musical journals. The success of the Steinway piano at the Paris Exposition of 1867 is recognized by this cartoonist.

The caption reads in translation:

The public at the exposition is suddenly seized with the rage to become pianist on hearing the admirable American Steinway pianos.

It will be noticed that the original lithograph was presented to the Steinways by the noted pianist, Vladimir Horowitz.

PLATE 96

Upright piano with Janko
keyboard made by Decker
Brothers, New York, c.
1890; compass AAA to c⁵,
two pedals: *una corda*, damper (Smithsonian Institu-
tion, 299,840, Hugo Worch
Collection). This was a
worthy attempt to aid the
pianist.

PLATE 97

Line drawing of the action of a modern grand piano. Well before the turn
of the century the mechanism of the American piano had achieved its
modern form in all essential details. It can be seen in this drawing that the
action of a modern grand piano is an awesome feat of engineering containing
nearly 12,000 individual parts. It was evolved over more than 200 years
through the combined ingenuity, imagination and labor of numerous
inventors and craftsmen.

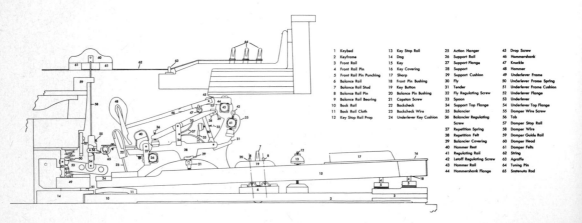

1 Keybed	13 Key Stop Rail	25 Action Hanger	45 Drop Screw
2 Keyframe	14 Dog	26 Support Rail	46 Hammershank
3 Front Rail	15 Key	27 Support Flange	47 Knuckle
4 Front Rail Pin	16 Key Covering	28 Support	48 Hammer
5 Front Rail Pin Punching	17 Sharp	29 Support Cushion	49 Underlever Frame
6 Balance Rail	18 Front Pin Bushing	30 Fly	50 Underlever Frame Spring
7 Balance Rail Stud	19 Key Button	31 Tender	51 Underlever Frame Cushion
8 Balance Rail Pin	20 Balance Pin Bushing	32 Fly Regulating Screw	52 Underlever Flange
9 Balance Rail Bearing	21 Capstan Screw	33 Spoon	53 Underlever
10 Back Rail	22 Backcheck	34 Support Top Flange	54 Underlever Top Flange
11 Back Rail Cloth	23 Backcheck Wire	35 Balancier	55 Damper Wire Screw
12 Key Stop Rail Prop	24 Underlever Key Cushion	36 Balancier Regulating	56 Tab
		Screw	57 Damper Stop Rail
		37 Repetition Spring	58 Damper Wire
		38 Repetition Felt	59 Damper Guide Rail
		39 Balancier Covering	60 Damper Head
		40 Hammer Rest	61 Damper Felts
		41 Regulating Rail	62 String
		42 Letoff Regulating Screw	63 Agraffe
		43 Hammer Rail	64 Tuning Pin
		44 Hammershank Flange	65 Sostenuto Rod

PLATE 98

Felt-covered hammers of a modern grand piano, tapered and graduated in size as developed from Jean-Henri Pape's ideas of 1839.

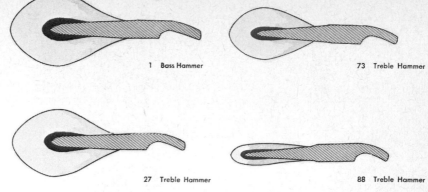

1 Bass Hammer

73 Treble Hammer

27 Treble Hammer

88 Treble Hammer

PLATE 99

(*caption overleaf*)

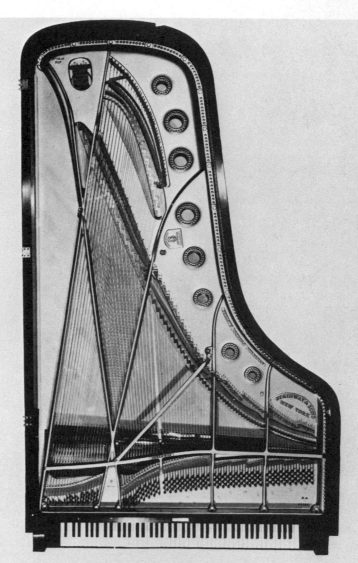

PLATE 99 (*preceding page, below*)

Frame of a modern concert grand. The cast-iron frame of a concert grand of today is built to withstand a tension of approximately 20 tons. The average tension of a single string is 165lb.

The diameters of the strings vary from approximately $\frac{1}{3}$in (including the copper over-spinning around the steel core) for the lowest to $\frac{1}{30}$in for the highest. The over-spinning or over-winding of the low strings was adopted as the keyboard compass was extended in order to lengthen the bass strings in correct proportion to the treble without making an impossibly long instrument. The lowest eight strings are single—one for each key—the next twelve are in pairs, and from thereon up each hammer strikes three steel strings. (Many early pianos were double-strung throughout.) The top twenty-one keys need no dampers, their vibrations being so small that it is unnecessary to subdue them.

The American concert grand is just under 9ft long. Bösendorfer of Austria makes, however, a grand that is 10ft long with a keyboard compass extended to eight octaves. All other keyboards remain at the compass adopted in the late nineteenth century: AAA to c⁵ or seven octaves plus a minor third.

The advantages of the grand over the upright shape lie in several areas. The floor under the former acts as a secondary soundboard, and the raised lid projects the sound in the direction of the audience whereas the upright is designed to be placed against a wall which is by nature acoustically dead. The hammers and dampers of a grand fall by gravity obviating the spring mechanism required for the upright. It hardly needs to be added that the grand shape is aesthetically more pleasing and the position of the performer in relation to the audience is more satisfactory.

PLATE 100 (*facing page*)

Concert grand piano by Steinway & Sons, New York, 1903; compass AAA to c⁵, three pedals: *una corda, sostenuto,* damper (on loan from the White House to the Smithsonian Institution, 379,287). This piano, the 100,000th made by Steinway, was presented to the United States government to commemorate fifty successful years of piano-making. It incorporates the metallic action frame patented in 1869, the repetition action, the *capo d'astro*[49] (or *capo tasto*) bar of 1875, the duplex scale of 1872 and the *sostenuto* pedal of 1874. This last, the middle or *sostenuto* pedal, here makes its only appearance in these illustrations. It was developed by Boisselot et Fils of Marseilles. When depressed with the left foot while one or more notes are struck, it permits these tones to continue sounding by immobilizing their raised dampers. At the same time other notes may be played and pedalled with the damper pedal as usual.

It was adopted by the Steinway firm in 1874, but it was never popular with European makers and was ignored or soon abandoned by them. It is seldom used and is considered a nuisance by some pianists. Josef Hoffman even had it removed from the pianos he used.

110

The case of the sumptuous piano illustrated here was designed by R. D. and J. H. Hunt. It is decorated with paintings by Thomas Dewing and with the seals of the original thirteen states on gold leaf background.

Its presence enhanced many a state occasion at the White House until it was replaced by the 300,000th Steinway made in 1938. It is now exhibited in the Smithsonian Institution in the First Ladies Hall.

7

STRINGED KEYBOARD INSTRUMENTS
TODAY

By the last quarter of the nineteenth century fine pianos were being made in many parts of the world. Among respected piano-makers in Germany were Bechstein, Blüthner, Grotrian-Steinweg;[50] in Austria Bösendorfer; in England Broadwood; in France Pleyel and Erard; in the United States Steinway, Chickering, Knabe, and Mason and Hamlin.

Iron framing, repetition action and tapered felt hammer covers were in universal use, and well before the turn of the century the keyboard compass of seven octaves plus a minor third (AAA to c^5) became standard.

Many of these nineteenth-century instruments are still in use and are cherished for their distinctive tonal quality. But serious makers have not been content to rest on their laurels, and constant experimentation for the 'ideal' piano continues. In the 1930s the Steinway firm patented its 'accelerated action' which is faster and more responsive than its predecessors. More recently it has added the 'perma-free action' intended to make the instrument more stable and durable in all changes of climate. In the 1960s the Baldwin company set out to make 'the most beautiful concert grand piano in the world' and to this end altered the lengths, gauges and layout of the strings, redesigned the bridge, and devised new pins for anchoring the strings to the metal frame. Its new instrument is much admired. Many more refinements are receiving consideration.

In the United States the peak year of popularity of the piano was 1909 when 364,545 pianos were purchased. Later the talking machine, motion pictures, the radio and other new forms of diversion caused it to fall from favor for some years, and the economic depression of the early thirties put some American makers out of business. Chickering, Knabe, and Mason and Hamlin were absorbed by other firms that continued using their names.

The piano, however, has slowly resumed its place of honor. From 107,000 various sizes and models shipped from manufacturers in the United States in 1937 the number rose to 208,941 in 1965, the highest in recent years.

More than 21,000,000 people now play the piano in the United States alone—about the same number as the combined total of all other instrumentalists.[51] The all-purpose musical instrument, the piano, is still considered basic for general training in music.[52]

Western piano-makers continue to prosper, and in Japan, the Nippon Gakki company, which produced its first piano as early as 1887, makes today an admirable piano, the Yamaha, in an enormous plant. With assembly-line methods, this turns out yearly an astonishing number of pianos along with a variety of other products, motorcycles included.

Renewed interest in the harpsichord parallels piano improvements.

The Pleyel piano firm made a few harpsichords in the 1880s and exhibited one at the Paris Exposition of 1889. Early in this century Wanda Landowska was including in her piano recitals a piece or two played on one of these instruments. They were not entirely satisfactory but Madame Landowska felt more and more strongly that harpsichord music should be played on a harpsichord rather than on a piano. After visiting European museums to see old instruments she conferred with Pleyel's chief engineer who drew up many plans for a new harpsichord and finally hit upon one that suited her. In 1912 she introduced her first large Pleyel harpsichord at a Bach festival. It was not a copy of an eighteenth-century instrument but it offered a similar sound; her performances revealed again the charm and beauty of music played on the type of instrument for which it was composed.

In the late 1880s in Paris, Louis Diémer, too, revived interest in the harpsichord, using in concerts a harpsichord made by Pascal Taskin in 1769 and which had remained in the Taskin family. In 1882 the owners had had it restored by Louis Tomasini and it was subsequently used by the Erard firm for study and as the basic design for its new model.

Arnold Dolmetsch must also receive special notice. A distinguished musician, French born, who had learned piano-making in his father's factory, he emigrated to England and, with a scholarly approach to the study of early instruments, built in 1894 his first clavichord and in 1895 his first harpsichord. In 1905 he was invited by Chickering & Sons to work at its plant in Boston and during the next four years made about seventy-five harpsichords. From 1911 to 1914 he produced some harpsichords for Gaveau in Paris, finally returning to England where his stringed keyboard instruments, lutes and viols, as well as his studies in early performance practices, aroused interest and admiration. The English pianist Violet Woodhouse was persuaded to try the Dolmetsch instruments and for many years, from about 1913, had a devoted following for her performances on his harpsichords and clavichords. An American pupil of Dolmetsch, John Challis, after study of clavichord- and harpsichord-making, set up his own workshop in Ypsilanti, Michigan, in the early 1930s, moving later to Detroit and to New York. He revived American interest in these instruments.

In time two schools of twentieth-century harpsichord-makers developed; one group builds instruments using modern techniques and materials in the interest of producing an instrument more rugged in construction and easier to maintain, and adding pedals to effect quick changes of registration. The other group, aspiring to recreate as faithfully as possible the baroque sound, uses great historical instruments as models.

The English and German makers, on the whole, belong to the first group. Frank Hubbard and William Dowd in the United States and Martin Skowroneck of Bremen, Germany, are outstanding representatives of the second group, making extraordinarily beautiful harpsichords that compete fairly with carefully restored early instruments. Many discerning musicians are turning to such instruments for performing harpsichord music. A pianist who has played the great harpsichord literature on a fine harpsichord may not find it practical to abandon the piano, but it is more than likely that he will approach the music differently as a result of the experience.

Just as by the end of the eighteenth century the piano was recognized as not an improved harpsichord but a new instrument, now in the twentieth century the harpsichord has been rediscovered as an instrument *sui generis* that the piano does not truly supplant. There is a growing inclination to prefer the harpsichord for the music composed for it and to reserve the piano for piano music, and some modern composers are even exploring the use of the harpsichord for expressing contemporary ideas. Interest is being shown too in rediscovering the expressive potential of the clavichord.

The piano itself has limitations that, if different from those of the harpsichord, are no less real. Like the harpsichord, however, it can be an eloquent and sensitive means of musical expression in the hands of a performer who accepts its limitations while fully exploiting its potentialities. Cristofori could not have dreamed of its subtleties of nuance and delicacy of control.

But what is the future of the piano? Some fine composers are now writing for the 'prepared' piano. For the performances of their compositions non-musical material such as paper, rubber bands, nuts and bolts, are applied to the strings (plate 101). The instrument is then played not only from the keyboard. The strings are plucked, struck with the hands or by other means, and the case itself is treated as a percussion instrument. The resulting sound is fascinating if not always 'musical' in the traditional sense.

It is not yet clear whether the prepared piano is a manifestation of dissatisfaction with the standard piano such as that for the harpsichord in the late eighteenth century, that will result in a totally new keyboard instrument, or whether it is a passing fad like the Janissary pedals.

In another direction increasing experimentation by serious musicians with electronic music arouses speculation that the piano as a basic instrument will become obsolete. Some feel that musical development in the future lies in the direction of quarter tones or even smaller fractions. Future keyboard instruments may have split keys to produce an increased number of tones within the octave like some seventeenth-century harpsichords (plate 36) and the piano by Johannes Zumpe mentioned on page 68; a few quarter-tone pianos made in Europe and the United States in the late nineteenth and early twentieth centuries have not received wide notice.

In the unlikely event of the piano being threatened by obsolescence, it is safe to assume, judging from the past, that makers will produce a new keyboard instrument or a major alteration of an existing type. So far, makers have risen successfully to challenges from composers and performers. At present, it appears that the piano is here to stay.

NOTES AND REFERENCES

1 Patricia Egan. 'Concert Scenes in Musical Paintings of the Italian Renaissance', *Journal of the American Musicological Society*, vol XIV, no 2 (Richmond, Va: William Byrd, summer 1961).

2 Representations of the early clavichord are known in Italian, German, Dutch, English, French and Yugoslavian works of art.

3 1428 is the date given by several respected authorities, although slightly later dates are assigned by some others. 1433 is the latest reasonable date offered.

4 Personal letter to author.

5 Edwin M. Ripin. 'The Early Clavichord', *The Musical Quarterly*, vol LIII (1967), 531–5. The technical matter of the difference in construction of the early and later clavichords would have no appropriate place here but for the interesting representations of the early type. The student of the subject will wish to refer to Mr Ripin's excellent article.

6 Italian: *clavicembalo, gravicembalo, cembalo, spinetta*; French: *clavecin, espinette, épinette*; German: *Cembalo, Kielflügel*.

7 The practice of designating pitches as 8′, 4′, 16′, 2′ is carried over from organ terminology. The 8′ pipe of the organ sounds C, the 4′ sounds c, the 16′ CC, and the 2′ c^1. See further explanation of pitch indications below:

AAA,BBB,CC,BB,C ,B, c , b ... $c^1 b^1 \; c^2 b^2 \; c^3 b^3 \; c^4 \quad b^4 c^5$

8 Also *eschiquier, eschaquier d'Angleterre* and in Spanish, *exaquier*.

9 *Les Traités d'Henri Arnault de Zwolle*, Bibliothèque Nationale MS BN Latin 7295. Facsimile edition, trans and ed by G. le Cerf and E. R. Labande (Paris: Edition August Picard, 1932), fol 128 ro, 5 (author's English translation).

10 Le Cerf and Labande. Introduction to *Les Traités d'Henri Arnault de Zwolle*.

11 Rosamond E. M. Harding. *The Piano-forte—Its History Traced to the Great Exhibition of 1851* (Cambridge, England: Cambridge University Press, 1933), p8, note 1.

12 *Les Traités d'Henri Arnault de Zwolle*. Note 5 (author's translation).

13 Opinions on the date and provenance are those of Mrs Elizabeth P. Wells, Curator of Instruments, Royal College of Music, London.

14 *Basso continuo*: see p48.

15 Facsimile edition (Kassel, Germany: Bärenreiter, 1966), vol 4, pp634–43.

16 Frank Hubbard. *Three Centuries of Harpsichord Making* (Cambridge, Mass: Harvard University Press, 1965), p105.

17 Figured bass: see p48.

18 Maffei mistakenly wrote the name as Cristofali.

19 Fabbri, Mario. 'Il primo "pianoforte" di Bartolomeo Cristofori', *Chigiana Rassegna Annuale di Studi Musicologici*, vol XXI ns I, 1960 (Florence, Italy: Olschki, 1964), 162–72.

20 E. F. Rimbault, trans. *The Pianoforte* (London: Robert Cocks 1860), p99.

21 Ralph Kirkpatrick. *Domenico Scarlatti* (Princeton, New Jersey: Princeton University Press, 1953), chap IX, pp178–85.

22 Abraham Rees, ed. 'Ravalement', *Cyclopaedia* (London: Longman, Hurst, Rees, Orme and Brom, c. 1805–19).

23 Emily Anderson, ed and trans. *The Letters of Mozart and His Family* (London: Macmillan, 1966).

24 Dénes Bartha, ed. *Joseph Haydn Gesammelte Briefe und Aufzeichnungen* (Kassel, Germany: Bärenreiter, 1965) (author's translation).

25 Compare with a Zumpe piano of 1767 in the Victoria & Albert Museum, London (W 27–1958).

26 The Mozart household contained several pianos by Fritz Späth of Regensburg.

27 Emily Anderson, ed and trans. Op cit.

28 Some American orchestras now tune to 442 and others in Europe as high as 456.

29 Harding. Op cit, appendix C, p317 and following.

30 Edouard Ganche. *Frédéric Chopin, sa vie et ses oeuvres*, p351 (author's translation).

31 Ibid.

32 Arthur Loesser. *Men, Women and Pianos* (New York: Simon & Schuster, 1954).

33 Ibid, p410.

34 Frank Hubbard with exquisite logic calls the keyboard with more than twelve notes to the octave 'nonenharmonic'; the term 'enharmonic' is customarily used.

35 Equal temperament was not universally adopted in Germany until c. 1800, in France and England c. 1850. It should be added that there are those who lament the abandonment of mean-tone temperament and a few are readopting it for the performance of early music. See John W. Link, Jr, 'The Promise of Meantone', *The Diapason* (January 1968).

36 Joseph Merlin was a Belgian inventor of extraordinary versatility. Among his inventions were a shorthand music-recording device attached to a harpsichord, a combined harpsichord and piano, a self-propelled invalid's chair, a pedal-operated tea table which caused the cups to rotate before the hostess, and roller skates.

37 Burney's six-octave piano has disappeared along with the harpsichord he mentions, but two other six-octave pianos by Merlin were still preserved in 1933 in England in the collection of Sir Albert Richardson.

38 F. C. Morse. *Furniture of the Olden Time* (New York: Macmillan, 1902), p262.

39 Harding. Op cit, appendix.

40 Personal letter from André Maurois, biographer of Hugo.

41 Author's translation.

42 Percy A. Scholes. *The Puritans and Music in England and New England* (New York: Russel & Russel, Inc, 1962), p36.

43 Pennsylvania Chapter of the Society of the Colonial Dames of America. *Church Music and Musical Life in Pennsylvania in the Eighteenth Century* (Lancaster, Pennsylvania: Wickersham Printing Co, 1926–47).

44 Daniel Spillane. *The History of the American Pianoforte* (New York: D. Spillane, 1790), p49.

45 Ibid, p76.

46 Hawkins was not only concerned with musical instruments; he was an indefatigable inventor. He once set up a short railway in Regent's Park, London, involving a railway, a carriage and horse and a differential pulley to demonstrate that with the aid of the pulley a horse could propel the carriage ten times as far as he moved. With Charles Wilson Peale, Hawkins patented a 'physiognatrace', capable of setting down on paper the outline of a person.

47 Only one other such Hawkins piano is known. It dates from 1800 and is in the collection of John Broadwood & Sons, London.

48 Louis Moreau Gottschalk. *Notes of a Pianist* (London: J. B. Lippincott, 1881).

49 The *capo d'astro* (or *capo tasto*) bar, like the agraffe, is for the purpose of securing the down-bearing of the bridge on the soundboard.

50 Founded by the son of Heinrich Engelhard Steinweg (Steinway), who stayed behind in Germany when the rest of the family came to the United States.

51 Statistics above provided by Steinway & Sons.

52 Even in Communist China in 1968 a piano was substituted for the first time for traditional gongs, cymbals and drums in a performance in Peking of the Chinese drama, *The Red Lantern*. Its use and the composition of the music for it were authorized, astonishingly and incongruously, by the Cultural Revolutionary Committee which issued the statement that the advantage of the piano is 'its wide range, its magnificent force and its varied ways of expression' that can bring into play 'the lofty and heroic images of the opera's characters'. The event *per se* is hardly of musical importance but it is striking evidence of the all-purpose nature of the piano and its continuing pervasion.

SELECTIVE BIBLIOGRAPHY

Anderson, Emily (trans). *The Letters of Mozart and His Family.* London: Macmillan, 1966

Apel, Willi. *Harvard Dictionary of Music.* Cambridge, Mass: Harvard University Press, 1962; rev and enlgd ed 1969

Arnault de Zwolle, Henri. *Instruments de musique du XVe siècle.* MS Fonds Latin 7295, Bibliothèque Nationale, Paris (Trans and ed G. Le Cerf and E. R. Labande. Paris: Editions Picard, 1932)

Bach, C. P. E. *Essay on the True Art of Playing Keyboard Instruments,* trans and ed William J. Mitchell. New York: W. W. Norton, 1949

Bédos de Celles, Dom François. *L'art du facteur d'orgues,* vol I. Paris: 1766 (Facsimile edition, Kassel, Germany: Bärenreiter, 1963)

Bessaraboff, Nicholas. *Ancient European Musical Instruments.* Cambridge, Mass: Harvard University Press, 1941

Boalch, Donald H. *Makers of the Harpsichord and Clavichord.* London: George Ronald, 1956

Bragard, Professor R. and DeHen, Dr Ferd J. *Les instruments de musique dans l'art et l'histoire.* Paris: Société Française du Livre, 1967. (Trans Bill Hopkins. *Musical Instruments in Art and History.* New York: Viking Press, 1968)

Brinsmead, Edgar. *The History of the Pianoforte with an Account of Ancient Music and Musical Instruments.* London, Paris and New York: Cassell, Petter & Galpin, 1877

Brown, Howard Mayer. *Instrumental Music Printed Before 1600.* Cambridge, Mass: Harvard University Press, 1965

Bruni, Antonio Bartolommeo. *Un inventaire sous la terreur. Etat des instruments de musique relevé chez les émigrés et les condamnés,* ed J. Galay. Paris: G. Chamerot, 1890

Buchner, Dr Alexander. *Musical Instruments through the Ages,* trans Iris Urwin. London: Spring Books, nd

Bukofzer, Manfred F. *Music in the Baroque Era.* New York: W. W. Norton, 1955

Bullock, Helen. *On Music in Colonial Williamsburg.* Williamsburg, Va: Dept of Research and Record, 1938

Chase, Gilbert. *America's Music.* New York: McGraw-Hill, 1955

Clemencic, René. *Old Musical Instruments,* trans David Hermges. New York: G. Putnam, 1968

Closson, Ernest. *History of the Piano,* trans Delano Ames. London: Paul Elek, 1947

Clutton, Cecil. 'The Pianoforte', *Musical Instruments through the Ages,* ed Anthony Baines. Baltimore: Pelican Books, 1969

Couperin, François. *L'art de toucher le clavecin.* Paris, 1717. (Reissued with English and German trans Leipzig: Breitkopf & Härtel, 1933)

——. *Pièces de clavecin.* Paris: Chez l'auteur, le sieur Foucaut, 1713–30

Dale, William. *Tschudi, the Harpsichord Maker.* London: Constable, 1913

Dart, Thurston. 'The Clavichord', *Musical Instruments through the Ages,* ed Anthony Baines. Baltimore: Pelican Books, 1969

David, Hans T. and Mendel, Arthur, eds. *The Bach Reader.* New York: W. W. Norton, 1945

Die Musik in Geschichte und Gegenwart, ed Friedrich Blume. Kassel, Germany: Bärenreiter, 1949–66

Dolge, Alfred. *Pianos and Their Makers.* Covina, Calif: Covina Publishing Company, 1911, and New York: Dover Books, 1972

Donington, Robert. *The Interpretation of Early Music.* New York: St Martins Press, 1963

Dufourg, Norbert, ed. *La Musique.* Paris: Larousse, 1965

Encyclopaedia Britannica. 11th ed, ed Hugh Chisholm. Cambridge, England: Cambridge University Press, 1910

Fabbri, Mario. 'Il primo "pianoforte" di Bartolomeo Cristofori', *Chigiana Rassegna Annuale di Studi Musicologici,* vol XXI, ns I. Florence, Italy: Olschki, 1964

Fay, Amy. *Music Study in Germany in the Nineteenth Century.* New York: Dover, 1965

Fithian, Philip Vickers. *The Journal and Letters of Philip Vickers Fithian,* ed and intro Hunter Dickinson Farish. Williamsburg, Va: Colonial Williamsburg, 1957

Galpin, Francis W. *Old Instruments of Music.* London: Methuen, 1910

Ganche, Edouard. *Frédéric Chopin, sa vie et ses oeuvres.* Paris: Mercure de France, 1921

Geiringer, Karl. *Haydn: A Creative Life in Music.* Berkeley, Calif: University of California Press, 1968

Goodwin, Mary. *Musical Instruments in Eighteenth Century Virginia.* Williamsburg, Va: Institute of Early American History and Culture, 1953

Gottschalk, Louis Moreau. *Notes of a Pianist.* London: J. P. Lippincott, 1881

Grove's Dictionary of Music, ed Eric Blom. 5th ed New York: St Martin's Press, 1959

Haake, Walter. *Am Klavier.* Königstein im Taunus, Germany: Hans Köster, 1968

Halfpenny, Eric. 'Music and Musical Instruments', *The Connoisseur Period Guide: The Georgian Period.* New York: Reynal, 1957

Hamilton, Clarence G. *Piano Music, Its Composers and Characteristics.* Boston: Oliver Ditson, 1925

Hanks, Sarah E. 'Pantaleon's Pantalon, an 18th Century Musical Fashion', *The Musical Quarterly,* vol LV, no 2. New York: G. Schirmer, April 1969

Harding, Rosamond E. M. *The Piano-forte—Its History Traced to the Great Exhibition of 1851.* Cambridge, England: Cambridge University Press, 1933. Reprinted New York: Da Capo Press, 1973

Harris, William Laurel. 'Musical Instruments as an Indication of Refinement and Culture', *Good Furniture,* vols VIII and IX. Grand Rapids, Michigan: Dean Hicks, January and July 1916

Harrison, Frank and Rimmer, Joan. *European Musical Instruments.* New York: W. W. Norton, 1964

Haydn, Joseph. *Gesammelte Briefe und Aufzeichnungen,* ed Dénes Bartha. Kassel, Germany: Bärenreiter, 1965

Hess, Albert G. 'The Transition from Harpsichord to Piano', *Gapin Society Journal,* vol VI. London: July 1953.

Hipkins, A. J. *A Descriptive History of the Pianoforte.* London: Novello Ewer, 1896

Hirt, Franz Joseph. *Meisterwerke des Klavierbaus.* Olten, Switzerland: Im Urs Graf-Verlag, 1955

Hollis, Helen. 'Jonas Chickering: The Father of American Pianoforte Making', *The Magazine Antiques*. New York, August 1973

——. *Pianos in the Smithsonian Institution*. Studies in History and Technology, no 27. Washington DC: Smithsonian Institution Press, 1973; rev ed 1974

Hoover, Cynthia A. *Harpsichords and Clavichords*. Washington DC: Smithsonian Institution Press, 1969

Howard, John Tasker. *The Music of George Washington's Time*. Washington DC: George Washington Bicentennial Commission, 1931

——. *Our American Music*. New York: Thomas Y. Crowell, 1965

Hubbard, Frank. *Three Centuries of Harpsichord Making*. Cambridge, Mass: Harvard University Press, 1965

James, Philip. *Early Keyboard Instruments*. New York: Frederick A. Stokes, 1930

Juramie, Ghislaine. *Histoire du piano*. Paris: Prisina, 1947

Kirkpatrick, Ralph. *Domenico Scarlatti*. Princeton, NJ: Princeton University Press, 1953

Krehbiel, Henry Edward. *The Pianoforte and Its Music*. New York: Scribner, 1911

Lesure, François. *Musik und Gesellschaft im Bild*. Kassel, Basel, Paris, London, New York: Bärenreiter, 1966. (Trans Denis and Sheila Stevens. *Music in Art and Society*. Philadelphia: Philadelphia State University Press, 1968)

Link, John W., Jr. 'The Promise of Meantone', *The Diapason*. Chicago, 1968

Loesser, Arthur. *Men, Women and Pianos*. New York: Simon & Schuster, 1954

Marcuse, Sibyl. *Musical Instruments: A Comprehensive Dictionary*. Garden City, New York: Doubleday, 1964

——. 'Transposing Keyboards on Extant Flemish Harpsichords', *The Musical Quarterly*. New York: G. Schirmer, July 1952

Meer, van der, John Henry. 'Beiträge zum Cembalobau in Deutschen Sprachgebeit bis 1700', *Anzeiger des Germanischen Nationalmuseums*, 1966

——. 'Review of *Three Centuries of Harpsichord Making* by Frank Hubbard', *Journal of the American Musicological Society*, vol XX, no 1 (spring 1967), 143–6

Mersenne, Marin. *Harmonie Universelle*. Facsimile edition. Paris: Centre National de la Recherche Scientifique, 1963

Morse, F. C. *Furniture of the Olden Times*. New York: Macmillan, 1902

Newman, William S. 'Beethoven's Piano versus His Piano Ideals', *Journal of the American Musicological Society*, vol XXIII, no 3 (autumn 1970), 484–504

Parrish, Carl. *The Early Piano and Its Influence on Keyboard Technique and Composition*. Harvard University thesis, 1939. Superior, Wis: Research Microfilm Publications, 1953

Pennsylvania Chapter of the Society of the Colonial Dames of America. *Church Music and Musical Life in Pennsylvania in the Eighteenth Century*. Lancaster, Pennsylvania: Wickersham Printing Co, 1926–47

Pepys, Samuel. *Diary and Correspondence of Samuel Pepys*, ed Rev Mynors Bright. New York: G. E. Croscup, 1892

Pirro, André. *Les Clavicinistes*. Paris: Laurens, 1925

Pols, André M. *De Ruckers en De Klavierbouw in Vlaandern*. Antwerp: N.V. De Nederlandsche, Roekhande, 1942

Rees, Abraham, ed. *The Cyclopaedia*. London: Longman, Hurst, Rees, Orme & Brown, 1819

Restout, Denise and Hawkins, Robert, eds. *Landowska on Music*. New York: Stein & Day, 1965

Reynvaan, Joos Verschuere. *Musykaal Kunst-Wordenboek*. Amsterdam, 1795

Rimbault, Edward B. *The Pianoforte*. London: Robert Cocks, 1860

Ripin, Edwin M. 'The Early Clavichord', *The Musical Quarterly*, vol LIII, no 4. New York: G. Schirmer, October 1967

——. 'The Two-Manual Harpsichord in Flanders Before 1650', *The Galpin Society Journal*, vol XXI. Chichester, Sussex: Phillimore, 1968

——. 'A Scottish Encyclopedist and the Piano Forte', *The Musical Quarterly*, vol LV, no 4. New York: G. Schirmer, October 1967

Russell, Raymond. *The Harpsichord and Clavichord*. London: Faber & Faber, 1959. Revised ed Howard Schott, New York: W. W. Norton, 1973

Sachs, Curt. *Das Klavier*. Berlin: J. Bard, 1923

——. *The History of Musical Instruments*. New York: W. W. Norton, 1940

Scholes, Percy A. *The Puritans and Music in England and New England*. New York: Russell & Russell, 1962

——. *The Great Dr Burney*. London: Oxford University Press, 1948

——. *The Oxford Companion to Music*. London: Oxford University Press, 1938

Shortridge, John D. *Italian Harpsichord Building in the 16th and 17th Centuries*. Washington DC: US National Museum Bulletin, no 225, 1960; rev ed 1970

Sitwell, Sacheverell. *Baroque and Rococo*. New York: G. Putnam, 1967

Spillane, Daniel. *History of the American Pianoforte*. New York: D. Spillane, 1890

Steinert, Morris. *Reminiscences of Morris Steinert*, comp and ed Jane Marlin. New York and London: G. Putnam, 1900

Straeten, Edmond van der. *La musique aux pays-bas avant le XIXe siècle*. Ghent, Belgium: A. et F. Mahillon, 1867–88

Strunk, Oliver, ed. *Source Readings in Music History*. New York: W. W. Norton, 1950

Sumner, W. L. *The Pianoforte*. London: MacDonald, 1966

Thayer, Alexander Wheelock. *The Life of Ludwig van Beethoven*, trans and ed H. E. Krehbiel. New York: The Beethoven Association, 1921–5

University of Edinburgh Faculty of Music. *The Russell Collection of Early Keyboard Instruments*. Edinburgh: University of Edinburgh, 1968

Virdung, Sebastian. *Musica Getutscht*. Basle: 1511. (Facsimile reprint, Berlin: Rob Eitner, 1882)

Winternitz, Emanuel. 'The Visual Arts as a Source for the Historian of Music', offprint from vol I, *IMS Congress Report*. Kassel, Basle, London, New York: Bärenreiter, 1961

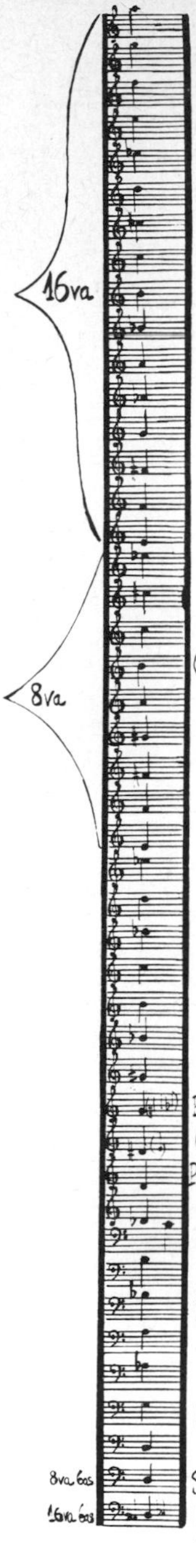

MATERIAL	STRINGS LEFT TO RIGHT	DISTANCE FROM DAMPER (INCHES)	MATERIAL	STRINGS LEFT TO RIGHT	DISTANCE FROM DAMPER (INCHES)	MATERIAL	STRINGS LEFT TO RIGHT	DISTANCE FROM DAMPER (INCHES)	TONE
			SCREW	2-3	1 1/4 *				A
			MED. BOLT	2-3	1 3/8 *				G
			SCREW	2-3	1 5/8 *				F
			SCREW	2-3	1 13/16 *				E
			SCREW	2-3	1 3/4 *				E♭
			SM. BOLT	2-3	2 *				D
			SCREW	2-3	1 11/16 *				C♯
			FURNITURE BOLT	2-3	2 3/16 *				C
			SCREW	2-3	2 1/2 *				B
			SCREW	2-3	1 7/8 *				B♭
			MED. BOLT	2-3	2 7/8 *				A
			SCREW	2-3	2 1/4 *				A♭
			SCREW	2-3	3 3/4 *				G
			SCREW	2-3	2 15/16 *				F♯
SCREW	1-2	3/4 *	FURN. BOLT + 2 NUTS	2-3	2 1/8 *	SCREW + 2 NUTS	2-3	3 1/4 *	F
			SCREW	2-3	1 13/16 *				E
			FURNITURE BOLT	2-3	1 7/8				E♭
			SCREW	2-3	1 15/16				C♯
			SCREW	2-3	1 1/16				C
(DAMPER TO BRIDGE = 4 7/16", ADJUST ACCORDINGLY)			MED. BOLT	2-3	3 3/4				B
			SCREW	2-3	4 7/16				A
RUBBER	1-2-3	4 1/2	FURNITURE BOLT	2-3	1 1/4				G♯
			SCREW	2-3	1 3/4				F♯
			SCREW	2-3	2 5/16				F
RUBBER	1-2-3	5 3/4							E
RUBBER	1-2-3	6 1/2	FURN. BOLT + NUT	2-3	6 7/8				E♭
			FURNITURE BOLT	2-3	2 9/16				D
RUBBER	1-2-3	3 5/8							D♭
			BOLT	2-3	7 1/8				C
			BOLT	2-3	2				B
SCREW	1-2	10	SCREW	2-3	1	RUBBER	1-2-3	8 1/4	B♭
(PLASTIC (see G))	1-2-3	2 15/16				RUBBER	1-2-3	4 1/2	G♯
PLASTIC (OVER 1 UNDER 2-3)	1-2-3	2 7/8				RUBBER	1-2-3	10 1/8	G
(PLASTIC (see D))	1-2-3	4 1/4				RUBBER	1-2-3	5 7/16	D♯
PLASTIC (OVER 1 - UNDER 2-3)	1-2-3	4 1/8				RUBBER	1-2-3	9 3/4	D
BOLT	1-2	15 1/2	BOLT	2-3	11/16	RUBBER	1-2-3	14 1/8	D♭
BOLT	1-2	14 1/2	BOLT	2-3	7/8	RUBBER	1-2-3	6 1/2	C
BOLT	1-2	14 3/4	BOLT	2-3	9/16	RUBBER	1-2-3	14	B
RUBBER	1-2-3	9 1/2	MED. BOLT	2-3	10 1/8				B♭
SCREW	1-2	5 7/8	LG. BOLT	2-3	5 7/8	SCREW + NUTS	1-2	1	A
BOLT	1-2	7 1/8	MED. BOLT	2-3	2 1/4	RUBBER	1-2-3	4 1/8	A♭
LONG BOLT	1-2	8 3/4	LG. BOLT	2-3	3 1/4				G
			BOLT	2-3	11/16				D
SCREW + RUBBER	1-2	4 7/16							D
ERASER (OVER D UNDER C♯ + E♭) AM. PENCIL CO. #346	1	6 3/4							D

* MEASURE FROM BRIDGE.

PLATE 101

Directions for preparing a piano for the John Cage work *Sonatas and Interludes* (Library of Congress).

INDEX

Accidentals, 38, 100, 101
Agraffe, invention of, 62
America, the piano in, 88–111
Arnault, Henri, 20, 26, 27, 29

Babcock, Alpheus, 89, 91, 102, 103
Bach, Carl Philipp Emanuel, 24, 55, 56; Johann Christian, 58; Johann Sebastian, 47, 49, 55, 68
Back-check, 52
Baroque music, 25, 39, 47
Beethoven, Ludwig van, 63, 64, 78, 80, 84, 95
Behaim, Lucas Friederich, 37
Behrent, John, 89
Bentsides, 31
Blanchet family, 43
Bortolotti, Alexander, 36
Broadwood, John, 41, 49, 57
Broken octave tuning, 38
Buntebart, Gabriel, 68
Burney, Charles, 72

Camerata, 47
Chamber music, 34, 89
Chickering, Jonas, 89, 91–3, 105; see also Osborn, John
Chopin, Frédéric, 62, 86
Chromatic keyboards, earliest, 27
Clavichords, 17–24
Clavicytherium, 30, 77, 79
Claviorganum, 36, 37
Clavisymbalom, 26, 27, 29, 48
Colombe, Jean, 29
Couperin, François, 49, 59
Crehore, Benjamin, 89
Cristofori, Bartolomeo, 51–4, 66
Cuntz, Stefan, 37

Damper system, 52, 66, 73
de Celles, Bedos, 36
de Zwolle, Henri Arnault, 20, 26, 27
Dolmetsch, Arnold, 113
Dulcimer, 11, 15, 29, 54
Dulcken, Johannes Daniel, 40

Échiquier (16th cent), 25, 26
Electronic music, 114
Elizabeth I, Queen, virginal of, 33
Erard, Sébastien, 61–2, 75, 79

Fretted instruments, 21, 23, 24

Geib, John, 58
Gottschalk, Louis Moreau, 94
Graf, Conrad, 64, 84
Gravicembalo, 52

Hammers, 109
Handel, George Frideric, 42, 49
Harding, Rosamond E. M., 29
Harmonic bar, invention of, 62
Harps, 11, 62
Harpsichords, 14th cent, 17; 15th to 18th cent, 25–46; transition from, to pianos, 47–50; in America, 88–9
Hass, Hieronymus Albrecht, and son, Johann, 44, 45, 46

Hawkins, John Isaac, 50, 90–1, 100, 101
Haydn, Joseph, 57, 63
Hebenstreit, Pantaleon, 54, 55
Henry VIII, King, instruments of, 33
Herz, Henri, 62
Hurdy-gurdy, 11, 16, 51

Iron frames, 92, 93, 94, 102, 107

Janissary sound, 95
Janko, *see* Von Janko, Paul
Jerome of Bologna, 39

Keyboards, chromatic, earliest, 27; dual and treble, 25; earliest, 22, 23; enharmonic, 38; Janko, 95, 96, 108; materials used in, 101; modern, 112–14; Moor-Duplex, 96; short-octave, 31
Knee levers, 43, 64, 73, 79

Liszt, Franz, 62, 63, 84, 85
Lutes, 29, 30, 32, 33

Maffei, Scipione, 52, 53, 55
Manichordian, 17
Marwinski, Konrad, 22
Mersenne, Marin, 51
Modern stringed keyboard instruments, 112–14
Monochord, 17, 48
Moravian orchestra, 88, 89
Mozart, father and sons, 42, 44; Wolfgang Amadeus, 42, 44, 57, 58, 63, 72, 95
Müller, Mathias, 90, 91

Nag's head swell, 50, 75

Octave couplers, 96
'Organisation', procedure for, 36
Organistrum (hurdy-gurdy), 11, 16
Organs, 11, 27, 37, 48; see also Portative organ
Osborn, John, 89, 91; see also Chickering, Jonas
Ottavino, 35, 36

Pachebel, Charles Theodore, 88
Pair, significance of, in instrumentality, 33
Pantaleons, 55
Pape, Jean-Henri, 83, 109
Pedal boards, 61, 73, 95
Pianists, 62–5
Pianos: action described, 52, 53; concert grand, 110; early experiments, 51; English action, 57–8, 70; French, 61–2; gadgets on, 95; giraffe, 80, 81; grand, 70, 86, 92, 94, 105; hammers, 109; harp-, 104; in America, 88–111; iron framed, 92, 93, 94, 102, 107; its earliest ancestors, 11–16; Janko keyboard, 95–6, 107; modern experiments, 94–6; modern instruments, 112–14; problems with, 59–61; pyramidal, 76; square, 58, 67, 75, 90, 99, 106; table, 83; transition to, from harpsichord, 47–50; upright,

82, 87, 90–1, 108; upright grands, 77; vertical, 61, 77; Viennese action, 58–9, 71; who invented?, 55, 56
Pitch lengths on harpsichord, 25, 40
Plectra, the making of, 25
Pleyel pianos, 62, 65, 87, 113
Portative organ, 15, 29
Prellemechanik, 59, 67
Prudde, John, 21, 28
Psaltery, 11, 12, 13, 14

Rebecs, 29
Reynvaan, 35
Ruckers family, 34, 35, 36, 40, 43
Rüffner, Gottlob, 67

St Cecilia, 27
Schmidt, Johann, 73
Schumann, Clara and Robert, 63, 86
Shakespeare, William, sonnet 128, 33
Shawms, 30
Short octave tuning and keyboard, 31
Shove coupler, 43
Shudi, Burkat (Burckardt Tschudi), 41, 42, 49
Silbermann, Gottfried, 54–6, 57, 59, 67
Söcher, Johann, 67
Sound, problems of increasing, in pianos, 60
Spinet, 25, 26, 39; differentiated from virginal, 39
Stehlin, Benoist, 43
Stein, Johann Andreas, 58–9, 69
Steinway & Sons, firm of, 86, 91, 93–4, 96, 106, 107, 110, 111
Stewart, James, 89, 92
Stodart, William, 77, 78
Stops, 40, 41, 49
Strings, details of, 110
Swells, 49, 50, 75, 100

Tabel, Hermann, 41
Taskin, Pascal, 43, 56, 73
Trilling, 25, 48, 60
Tuning: broken octave, 38; equal temperament, 38; *ottavino*, pitch lengths, 25, 40; short octave, 31; whole-tone scale, 95
Turkish influence, 95
Twilight era, 56–7

Una corda device, 66, 79, 80, 106
Unfretted instruments, 24

Van Eyck, Hubert and Jan, 27
Venetian swell, 49, 50, 100
Viola da gamba, 32, 34, 37
Virginal, 25, 26, 31–4, 38; double, 35, 36; differentiated from spinet, 39
Von Falckenburg, Friedrich, 37
Von Janko, Paul, 95, 96, 107

Wissmayr, Paul, 37
Wornum, Robert, 82

Xylophone, with keys, 51

Zumpe, Johannes, 57–8, 61, 68